EP Literature and Composition II Language Arts

This book belongs to:

_____

EP Literature and Composition II Language Arts

About this Book

This is an offline version of the language arts selections of Easy Peasy All-in-One High School's Literature and Composition II course. We've modified and expanded upon the online activities and printable worksheets available at the Easy Peasy All-in-One High School website (allinonehighschool.com) so that you can work offline if desired. This book is ONLY the language arts component of Literature and Composition II. It will not include any of the reading or vocabulary assignments and is not a complete English course on its own.

How to use this Book

This book is designed to be used in conjunction with the Literature and Composition II Reading and Vocabulary books (for a full offline course) OR alongside the online Literature and Composition II course. As you proceed through this book, you will use the other Literature and Composition II workbooks or the online assignments to fill out the rest of the assignments.

This book follows the EP online Literature and Composition II course in sequential order, providing an offline version of the language arts assignments. A student completing the assignments in this book along with the other Literature and Composition II workbooks or the other online assignments will complete one full high school English course.

Course Description: Language Arts Portion

Students will focus this year on analyzing literature, including poetry, short stories, novels, and plays. Students will develop their understanding of literary devices and terminology to be able to express researched critiques of literature. Students will produce a number of literary analysis papers as well as other essays. Additionally, students will be engaged creatively in writing short stories and poetry. Students will use the complete writing process. Students will also read a variety of nonfiction and will be expected to produce a newspaper as part of their nonfiction studies. To improve in their writing, students will study spelling, vocabulary, grammar, suspense, irony, metaphor, theme, mood, and foreshadowing. Students will take a final exam at the end of the course.

PLEASE NOTE We would encourage you to find a peer-editing partner. On Lessons 35 and 105, students will be instructed to give their paper to someone else to read in order to get feedback. Ideally, this would be someone in their same grade that they could reciprocate with, but they should have someone who can read it and provide feedback.

You may want to consider taking the Analyzing and Interpreting Literature CLEP test after this course. If you pass, you would get college credit. You could also label this as an honors course.

Completion Chart for Lessons 1 - 45

№		№		№	
(1)	review	(16)	analyzing poetry	(31)	short story sequence/terms
(2)	MLA format	(17)	literary analysis/ archetypes	(32)	irony/ foreshadowing
(3)	plagiarism	(18)	passive voice	(33)	compare and contrast essay
(4)	evaluating sources	(19)	passive voice	(34)	irony
(5)	literary analysis	(20)	passive voice	(35)	compare and contrast essay
(6)	literary analysis	(21)	active and passive voice	(36)	compare and contrast essay
(7)	MLA format	(22)	no assignment	(37)	compare and contrast essay
(8)	sentence fragments/ run-ons	(23)	no assignment	(38)	the Trojan War
(9)	poetic devices	(24)	literary analysis	(39)	essay/*The Odyssey*
(10)	analyzing poetry	(25)	no assignment	(40)	essay/*The Odyssey*
(11)	imitating poetic devices	(26)	literary analysis	(41)	short story/*The Odyssey*
(12)	sentence fragments/ run-ons	(27)	literary analysis	(42)	short story/*The Odyssey*
(13)	poetic devices	(28)	literary analysis	(43)	short story/*The Odyssey*
(14)	analyzing poetry	(29)	literary analysis	(44)	short story/*The Odyssey*
(15)	symbolism/ analyzing poetry	(30)	literary analysis	(45)	short story/*The Odyssey*

Completion Chart for Lessons 46 - 90

(46)	*The Odyssey/ verb tense agreement*	(61)	*The Odyssey study guide*	(76)	journal prompt
(47)	*The Odyssey study guide*	(62)	*The Odyssey study guide*	(77)	journal prompt
(48)	*The Odyssey study guide*	(63)	*The Odyssey matching*	(78)	journal prompt
(49)	*The Odyssey/ journal prompts*	(64)	*The Odyssey test*	(79)	no assignment
(50)	*The Odyssey/ journal prompts*	(65)	journal prompt	(80)	journal prompt
(51)	*The Odyssey/ journal prompts*	(66)	*The Odyssey essay question*	(81)	journal prompt
(52)	*The Odyssey/ journal prompts*	(67)	no assignment	(82)	journal prompt
(53)	*The Odyssey/ journal prompts*	(68)	journal prompt	(83)	journal prompt
(54)	*The Odyssey/ journal prompts*	(69)	newspaper project	(84)	journal prompt
(55)	*The Odyssey/ journal prompts*	(70)	newspaper project	(85)	journal prompt
(56)	*The Odyssey study guide/ letter*	(71)	newspaper project	(86)	journal prompt
(57)	*The Odyssey study guide*	(72)	pronouns	(87)	journal prompt
(58)	*The Odyssey study guide*	(73)	pronouns	(88)	journal prompt
(59)	*The Odyssey study guide*	(74)	pronouns	(89)	journal prompt
(60)	*The Odyssey study guide*	(75)	pronouns	(90)	essay

Completion Chart for Lessons 91-135

#		#		#	
91	essay	106	irregular plurals/possessives	121	newspaper project
92	essay	107	story elements	122	sentence structures
93	essay	108	no assignment	123	poetic devices
94	essay/parallel form	109	short story	124	descriptive writing
95	nonfiction	110	short story	125	analyzing poetry
96	nonfiction/biography	111	short story	126	descriptive writing
97	biography	112	short story	127	poem assignment
98	biography	113	short story/"A Hunger Artist" quiz	128	poetic devices/poetry notebook
99	parallelism/biography	114	literary analysis	129	poetry notebook project
100	journal prompt	115	short story terms quiz	130	poetry notebook project
101	MLA formatting	116	newspaper project	131	poetry notebook project
102	citing sources/literary terms	117	newspaper project	132	poetry notebook project
103	literary analysis	118	newspaper project	133	no assignment
104	plurals and possessives	119	newspaper project	134	no assignment
105	biography	120	newspaper project	135	no assignment

Completion Chart for Lessons 136-180

(136)	no assignment	(151)	no assignment	(166)	journal prompt
(137)	no assignment	(152)	*Emma* quiz	(167)	no assignment
(138)	no assignment	(153)	iambic pentameter/ analysis	(168)	no assignment
(139)	no assignment	(154)	malapropism	(169)	fable chart/fable writing
(140)	no assignment	(155)	*Much Ado About Nothing* writing	(170)	fable chart/fable writing
(141)	no assignment	(156)	*Much Ado About Nothing* writing	(171)	no assignment
(142)	short story/subject-verb agreement	(157)	*Much Ado About Nothing* writing	(172)	nonfiction writing
(143)	no assignment	(158)	*Much Ado About Nothing* writing	(173)	final exam study
(144)	no assignment	(159)	*Much Ado About Nothing* writing	(174)	final exam study
(145)	no assignment	(160)	*Much Ado About Nothing* writing	(175)	final exam study
(146)	poetry/prepositional phrases	(161)	*Much Ado About Nothing* writing	(176)	final exam study
(147)	no assignment	(162)	*Much Ado About Nothing* writing	(177)	final exam study
(148)	no assignment	(163)	*Much Ado About Nothing* quiz	(178)	final exam study
(149)	no assignment	(164)	*Much Ado About Nothing* writing	(179)	final exam study
(150)	no assignment	(165)	editing/nonfiction terms	(180)	final exam

Grading Sheet: Quarter 1

Record your scores on the sheet below as the assignments instruct you to do so.

Date	Lesson	Assignment	My Score	Possible Score
	3	Plagiarism Quiz		5
	4	Online Sources Quiz		5
	5	Vocabulary Quiz: Unit 1		10
	5	Literary Terms Quiz		5
	10	Vocabulary Quiz: Unit 2		10
	11	Imitating Poetic Devices		25
	15	Vocabulary Quiz: Unit 3		10
	16	Analyzing Poetry Project		100
	25	Vocabulary Quiz: Unit 4		10
	30	Vocabulary Quiz: Unit 5		10
	31	Literary Analysis		100
	34	Irony Examples		9
	35	Vocabulary Quiz: Unit 6		10
	35	Irony Chart		5
	35	Foreshadowing Chart		5
	40	Compare/Contrast Initial Essay		25
	40	Compare/Contrast Feedback		25
	40	Compare/Contrast Final		100
	45	Vocabulary Quiz: Unit 7		10
	45	Short Story		80
		TOTAL		

Grading Sheet: Quarter 2

Record your scores on the sheet below as the assignments instruct you to do so.

Date	Lesson	Assignment	My Score	Possible Score
	46	Verb Tense Agreement Quiz		25
	49	Journal Prompt		5
	50	Vocabulary Quiz: Unit 8		10
	50	Journal Prompt		5
	51	Journal Prompt		5
	52	Journal Prompt		5
	53	Journal Prompt		5
	54	Journal Prompt		5
	55	Journal Prompt (Extra credit)		0
	55	Vocabulary Quiz: Unit 9		10
	56	Letter to Penelope		10
	64	*The Odyssey* Test and Reading		50
	65	Vocabulary Quiz: Unit 10		10
	65	Journal Prompt		5
	66	*The Odyssey* Essay Question		10
	68	Journal Prompt		5
	70	Vocabulary Quiz: Unit 11		10
	71	Newspaper Article		100
	75	Vocabulary Quiz: Unit 12		10
	76	Journal Prompt		5
	77	Journal Prompt		5
	78	Journal Prompt		5
	80	Journal Prompt		5
	81	Journal Prompt		5
	82	Journal Prompt		5
	83	Journal Prompt		5
	84	Journal Prompt		5
	85	Vocabulary Quiz: Unit 13		10
	85	Journal Prompt		5
	86	Journal Prompt		5
	87	Journal Prompt		5
	88	Journal Prompt		5
	89	Journal Prompt		5
	90	Vocabulary Quiz: Unit 14		10
		TOTAL		

Grading Sheet: Quarter 3

Record your scores on the sheet below as the assignments instruct you to do so.

Date	Lesson	Assignment	My Score	Possible Score
	94	Camelot/Kennedy Essay		100
	94	Parallel Form		9
	95	Vocabulary Quiz: Unit 15		10
	100	Journal Prompt		5
	102	Plagiarism Quiz		5
	102	Literary Terms Quiz		5
	105	Biography		100
	106	Plurals and Possessives Quiz		25
	110	Vocabulary Quiz: Unit 16		10
	113	"A Hunger Artist" Quiz		4
	115	Vocabulary Quiz: Unit 17		10
	115	Short Story Terms Quiz		6
	116	Short Story Original Score		50
	116	Short Story Peer Edit Score		25
	116	Short Story Redo Score		50
	120	Vocabulary Quiz: Unit 18		10
	121	Newspaper Project		125
	122	Sentence Structure Quiz		10
	126	Descriptive Writing Assignment		50
	127	Poem Assignment		50
	130	Vocabulary Quiz: Unit 19		10
	132	Poetry Notebook Project		105
	135	Vocabulary Quiz: Unit 20		10
		TOTAL		

Grading Sheet: Quarter 4

Record your scores on the sheet below as the assignments instruct you to do so.

Date	Lesson	Assignment	My Score	Possible Score
	140	Vocabulary Quiz: Unit 21		10
	142	Subject/Verb Agreement Quiz		25
	150	Vocabulary Quiz: Unit 22		10
	152	*Emma* Quiz		10
	153	Iambic Pentameter		25
	155	Vocabulary Quiz: Unit 23		10
	158	Character Writing		5
	159	*Much Ado About Nothing* Topic		10
	160	Vocabulary Quiz: Unit 24		10
	160	Class Discussion Question		5
	160	*Emma* Literary Analysis		100
	161	Class Discussion Question		5
	162	Play Summary		5
	163	*Much Ado About Nothing* Quiz		10
	163	*Much Ado About Nothing* Topic		10
	164	*Much Ado About Nothing* Topic 1		10
	164	*Much Ado About Nothing* Topic 2		10
	166	Journal Prompt		5
	172	Fable Assignment		100
	179	Non-Fiction Writing Assignment		60
	180	Final Exam		100
		TOTAL		

Let's do some grammar review. First, read through this list of commonly mixed up words. You might want to highlight or mark the ones that cause you confusion, revisiting the list often until you learn the correct usage of each word. If you constantly struggle with a group of words that aren't on this list, add them and study them until you're using them correctly.

accent – pronunciation specific to a region
ascent – rising or climbing
assent – agreement

accept – receive
except – not including

adverse – unfavorable
averse – opposed to

advice – guidance
advise – to recommend

affect – (v) influence
effect – (n) result; (v) to cause

aisle – a passage between rows
isle – an island

a lot – many
allot – portion out

all ready – completely prepared
already – by now

all together – in one place
altogether – completely

allude – hint at
elude – avoid

allusion – passing reference
illusion – deceptive appearance

altar – a sacred place
alter – change

angel – spiritual messenger of God
angle – the space between two intersecting lines or shapes

are – plural form of "to be"
our – plural form of "my"

assistance - help
assistants - helpers

bare – naked
bear – (n) an animal; (v) to carry

beside – next to
besides – except for; in addition

boar – wild male pig
bore – drill a hole through

board – a piece of wood
bored – disinterested

born – brought into life
borne – carried

brake – device used for stopping
break – destroy

breath – air that's taken in
breathe – to take in air

buy – purchase
by – next to; through the agency of
bye – break in competition; short for goodbye

canvas – heavy cloth
canvass – a survey or to take a survey

capital – major city
capitol – government building

choose – pick
chose – past tense of "to choose"

cite – to document or quote
sight – something that is seen
site – place or location; website

clothes – garments
cloths – pieces of fabric

coarse – rough
course – path; class or series of lectures

complement – something that completes
compliment – praise

conscience – sense of morality
conscious – awake

corps – regulated group
corpse – dead body

council – governing body
counsel – (v) give advice; (n) advice

dairy – place that processes milk products
diary – personal journal

descent – moving downward
dissent – disagreement

desert – (n) dry, sandy area; (v) abandon
dessert – sweet, final course in a meal

device – a tool; a plan
devise – create

dew – water droplets condensed from air
do – perform or execute something
due – as a result of; owed

die – to lose life; a single of a pair of dice
dye – to change or add color

discreet – modest behavior
discrete – distinct, separate thing

dominant – commanding, controlling
dominate – to control

dyeing – changing or adding color
dying – losing life

elicit – to draw out
illicit – illegal or forbidden

envelop – to surround
envelope – container for a letter

every day – each day
everyday – ordinary

fare – money for transportation; food
fair – (adj) just; light skinned; (n) carnival

farther – at a greater distance
further – in more depth

formally – officially; with ceremony
formerly – previously

forth – forward
fourth – number four in a sequence

gorilla – animal in the ape family
guerilla – soldier known for sneak attacks

hear – sense sound
here – this place

heard – past tense of "hear"
herd – group of animals

hole – opening
whole – complete; entire thing

human – person; homo sapien
humane – compassionate

it's – contraction for it is
its – possessive form of "it"

knew – past tense of "know"
new – fresh, not old

know – comprehend
no – negative

later – after a time
latter – second of two things

lead – guide; heavy metal substance
led – past tense of "to lead"

lessen – decrease
lesson – something learned or taught

lightning – storm-related electricity
lightening – making lighter

loose – not tightly fastened
lose – to misplace

maybe – perhaps
may be – might be

meat – animal flesh
meet – encounter
mete – measure; distribute

medal – flat disk with design; prize
metal – hard organic substance
mettle – courage, energy

miner – a worker in a mine
minor – (n) underage person; (adj) less important

moral – distinguishing right from wrong; lesson of a story
morale – attitude or outlook

passed – past tense of "pass"
past – at a previous time

patience – putting up with annoyances
patients – people under medical care

peace – absence of war
piece – part of a whole; musical number

peak – top point, pinnacle
peek – look or peer through
pique – a feeling of resentment

pedal – foot lever of a bike or car
peddle – sell
petal – segment of a flower

personal – intimate; owned by someone
personnel - employees

plain – simple
plane – (n) aircraft; (v) to shave wood

precede – come before
proceed – continue

presence – attendance; being at hand
presents – gifts

principal – (adj) foremost; (n) school administrator
principle – moral conviction; basic truth

quiet – silent, not loud
quite – very

rain – (n) falling water drops; (v) the act of water drops falling
reign – to rule
rein – (n) the strap to control an animal; (v) guide or control

raise – to lift up
raze – to tear down

rational – having reason
rationale – beliefs

respectfully – with respect
respectively – in that order

reverend – title given to clergy
reverent – worshipful

right – correct; opposite of left
rite – ritual, ceremony
write – put words on paper

road – path
rode – past tense of "ride"

scene – place of action; section of a play
seen – viewed; past participle of "see"

sense – understanding or perception
since – because; measurement of past time

stationary – still
stationery – paper

straight – unbending
strait – a waterway; narrow

taught – past tense of "teach"
taut – tight

than – besides; used for comparison
then – at that time; next

their – possessive form of "they"
there – in that place
they're – contraction for "they are"

threw – past tense of "throw"
thorough – complete
through – finished; into and out of

to – toward
too – also; very (emphasis)
two – number after one

track – course, road
tract – plot of ground; pamphlet

waist – midsection of the body
waste – (n) discarded material; (v) squander

waive – forgo
wave – movement of the ocean; flutter

weak – not strong
week – seven days

wear – have on the body
were – past tense of "to be"
where – in which place

weather – climatic condition
whether – if

which – one of a group
witch – female sorcerer

who's – contraction for "who is"
whose – possessive for "of who"

you're – contraction for "you are"
your – possessive for "of you"
yore – time long past

Lesson 1: Punctuation Marks

Review punctuation marks and when they are used.

- **Period .**
  - o Ends a sentence flatly

- **Question mark ?**
  - o Ends a sentence with curiosity

- **Exclamation mark !**
  - o Ends a sentence with excitement

- **Asterisk ***
  - o Suggests further comment or clarification

- **En dash -**
  - o Replaces the word "through" or "to" when suggesting a time duration

- **Semicolon ;**
  - o Joins two related, complete sentences
  - o Separates list items when commas are in the list

- **Brackets [ ]**
  - o Indicate comments by someone other than the author
  - o Indicate parenthetical information already in parentheses

- **Parentheses ( )**
  - o Suggest related but unnecessary information
  - o Clarify something
  - o Indicate page references or citations of some kind

- **Ellipsis …**
  - o Indicates an omission or words in a quote
  - o Indicates hesitation in speech in a dialogue
  - o Suggests that something is being left out

- **Em Dash —**
  - o Expands a main clause with emphasis
  - o Separates special ideas and draws attention to them
  - o Suggests a change in direction or interruption in thought

- **Quotation marks " "**
  - Indicates dialogue
  - Indicates a quotation of another source
  - Suggests sarcasm
  - Highlights a word
  - Indicates short pieces of media like poems, songs, articles, etc.

- **Colon :**
  - Expands or clarifies a main clause
  - Introduces a list
  - Follows a greeting or salutation
  - Separates hours from minutes
  - Separates titles from subtitles
  - Indicates dialogue in a play
  - Used to show ratios

- **Hyphen -**
  - Creates a compound adjective
  - Combines two-digit numbers
  - Clarifies verbs with common prefixes
  - Joins a prefix to a capitalized word
  - Joins a letter or number to a word
  - Joins a prefix to a date
  - Separates words with the same three letters in a row

- **Apostrophe '**
  - Indicates a quote within a quote
  - Omits letters and numbers
  - Creates a plural for a single letter
  - Used in making nouns and abbreviations possessive

- **Comma ,**
  - Separates items in a list
  - Separates coordinate adjectives
  - Separates coordinating conjunctions
  - Separates dependent clauses
  - Separates appositives
  - Comes after introductory phrases
  - Comes after interjections
  - Comes after a direct address
  - Comes after a title
  - Separates the day and month from the year in a date
  - Separates numbers four digits and larger
  - Separates cities from states
  - Comes after abbreviations i.e. and e.g.
  - Comes before quotations

Finally, review these MLA terms and definitions. Make sure you know what they all mean. You can quiz yourself or have someone else read the terms to you while you supply the definitions. *(This is the end of Lesson 1 in this book. Be sure to also complete Lesson 1 in your Reader and your Vocabulary Workbook.)*

Thesis Statement: One sentence that appears at the end of the introduction and reveals the main idea of the essay.

Topic Sentence: A sentence that reveals what the body paragraph will be about.

Introduction Paragraph: The first paragraph of an essay that introduces the main idea of the essay and ends with the thesis statement.

Body Paragraph: The main part of your essay or paper. Each body paragraph contains a topic sentence that tells readers what the paragraph is going to be about, supporting sentences that discuss the idea or ideas in the topic sentence using examples and/or evidence to support that discussion and a concluding sentence that emphasizes the importance of the supporting examples or evaluates the connections between them.

Conclusion Paragraph: The final paragraph in the essay that provides a call to action and not a summary. The conclusion paragraph should give your readers something to think or discuss about the points in the essay.

Development Sentence: Occurs after the topic sentence in the body paragraph and provides a perspective on the topic that will allow for an understanding of the importance of the evidence that will follow—your opinion, thought, or idea regarding the topic.

Evidence: All words, ideas, facts, or data from another source (other than the brain) that backs up the statements and opinions expressed—must be cited.

Analysis Sentence: Explains why the evidence is important and how it connects to the thesis—do not restate or summarize the evidence.

Conclusion Sentence: Last sentence in the paragraph that draws the body paragraph to a close.

In-Text Citation: The short version of the Source Citation that appears directly after the evidence used and refers the reader to the longer Source Citation.

Source Citation: Publication information in a specific formula for a source used for evidence in a piece of writing

Works Cited: A list of all source citations of the sources used in a piece of writing.

Lesson 2: MLA Format

Refresh your memory on MLA format. If you'd like to see an example paper, there is one linked in Lesson 2 of the online course.

- An MLA paper needs to be typed on a computer and printed on white 8.5x11-inch paper.
- The paper should be double-spaced and in a legible font. Sans serif fonts are the most legible (such as Times New Roman). You should use 12 pt. font.
- There should only be one space after periods or other punctuation marks.
- The margins of an MLA paper should be 1 inch on all sides.
- The first line of each paragraph should be indented a half-inch from the left margin. In MLA, it is suggested that you use the "Tab" key on your keyboard, rather than hitting your spacebar five times.
- An MLA paper should have page numbers in the upper right-hand corner, preceded by your last name. You'll want to place this in the header space so that it's a half-inch from the top of the page and flush with the right margin of the paper.
- Italics should be used throughout your paper to indicate titles and, if necessary, to provide emphasis.
- If the paper has section headings, they should be numbered with a numeral followed by a period, and then a space and the section name in title case, or the proper capitalization used for titles. (1. Before the Ball)
- Endnotes, if any, should be included on a separate page before the Works Cited page. This page should have the centered title Notes.
- Unless you're asked to make a title page, the first page should just begin the paper. The upper left-hand corner of the first page should have your name, your instructor's name, the course, and the date all on separate lines and double-spaced.
- Double-spaced and centered beneath those things should be the title written in title case, not all caps. Do not underline, italicize, or otherwise format your title.
- Do use italics or quotation marks in the title if you're referring to other works, just like you would in the body of your paper (for example: Situational Irony in *The Necklace*).
- Double-space between the title and the first line of your paper.

You'll want to know the basics of MLA formatting, but you can always look up anything you have a question about as you're writing a paper. Literature and Composition I had many lessons on MLA formatting if you need to review. A good page to bookmark on your computer for help with MLA formatting is: https://rht102.wordpress.com/resources/

Here's an example of a proper first page:

Tina Rutherford

Professor Barbara Byers

English 101

21 May 2021

Situational Irony in *The Necklace*

 My first line is indented and now I'm going to share my introduction. It should include my thesis statement. I'm just filling this paragraph out for an example. I'm just filling this paragraph out for an example. I'm just filling this paragraph out for an example. I'm just filling this paragraph out for an example. I'm just filling this paragraph out for an example. I'm just filling this paragraph out for an example.

 I'm just filling this paragraph out for an example. I'm just filling this paragraph out for an example. I'm just filling this paragraph out for an example. I'm just filling this paragraph out for an example. I'm just filling this paragraph out for an example. I'm just filling this paragraph out for an example, I'm just filling this paragraph out for an example. I'm just filling this paragraph out for an example. I'm just filling this paragraph out for an example. I'm just filling this paragraph out for an example.

 I'm just filling this paragraph out for an example. I'm just filling this paragraph out for an example. I'm just filling this paragraph out for an example. I'm just filling this paragraph out for an example. I'm just filling this paragraph out for an example. I'm just filling this paragraph out for an example. I'm just filling this paragraph

Here's a refresher about how to cite your sources. You can briefly scan this information (pay attention to the in-text citations as well) and then come back to this lesson when you need to put the information to use.

Works Cited page

- Your Works Cited page will begin on a new page at the very end of your paper. The title Works Cited should be centered (do not italicize the words Works Cited or put them in quotation marks). Everything else will be aligned to the left margin of your paper.

- All citations will be double-spaced like the rest of your paper, but there should not be an extra space between citations.

- Any citations that take up more than one line should have the second and any subsequent lines indented half an inch to create a hanging indent, like this:

  > Duckworth, Brittany Bartel. "Getting Along With Your Siblings." *Brio*, vol. 21, no. 3, 2017, pp. 24-5.

- When listing page numbers, use pp. if multiple page numbers were used, and p. if single pages were used. In MLA, you also omit the first sets of repeated digits (as seen in the above example. Pages 24-25 were marked as pp. 24-5. Pages 335-365 would be written pp. 335-65.

- The entries on your page should be listed alphabetically by author's last name. If an entry does not have a known author, they're included alphabetized by their title as that's the first part of their citation. So you might have sources listed like this:

  > Brown, Jim. *The*...
  > *Causes of Anxiety*.
  > Delphia, Cindy. "The…

- When creating your Works Cited page, no matter the publication, there is a specific order and punctuation to the information. It should follow this order (not all items will apply to each work you're citing. Just skip in order down to the next one you need).
  - Author.
  - Title of source.
  - Title of container,
  - Other contributors,
  - Version,
  - Number,
  - Publisher,
  - Publication date,
  - Location.

    - Begin with the **author**'s last name, a comma, and the rest of the name as the work presents it. End the entire portion with a period.
      - Peretti, Frank. *The Oath*. Word Publishing, 1999.

    - The **title of your source** should follow the author's name. The type of source will determine whether it's italicized or in quotation marks.
      - Italicize titles of books, plays, films, periodicals, databases, and websites.
        - Peretti, Frank. *The Oath*. Word Publishing, 1999.
          - The title of the book is italicized

      - Use quotation marks around articles, essays, chapters, poems, webpages, songs, speeches, and anything else that is part of a larger work.

- Homolka, "Perfect Air Fryer Chicken Breast – No Breading." *SkinnyTaste*, www.skinnytaste.com/air-fryer-chicken-breast.
  - The individual webpage is in quotation marks; the name of the parent site is in italics.

- Duckworth, Brittany Bartel. "Getting Along With Your Siblings." *Brio*, vol. 21, no. 3, 2017, pp. 24-25.
  - The article title is in quotation marks while the magazine name is in italics.

- Chapman, Steven Curtis. "Much of You." *All Things New*, Sparrow Records, 2004, www.music.apple.com/us/album/all-things-new/716357999
  - The song title is in quotation marks and the album title is in italics.

- The **title of your container**, if applicable, comes next. Containers are larger wholes which contain the source. For instance, if you cite a poem that is found within a collection of poems, the poem is your source and the collection is the container. In the above three examples, the container is the italicized portion directly following the title.
  - You can also have more than one container. Perhaps you watched an episode of Parks and Recreation on Netflix. The episode is your source. The container is the series. But another container is Netflix. Here's how that would look.
    - "94 Meetings." *Parks and Recreation*, season 2, episode 21, *NBC*, 29 Apr. 2010. *Netflix*, www.netflix.com/watch/70152031?trackId=200256157&tctx=0%2C20%2C0974d361-27cd-44de-9c2a-2d9d868b9f64-12120962.

- **Other contributors** include those listed other than authors such as editors, illustrators, and translators.
  - Foucault, Michel. *Madness and Civilization: A History of Insanity in the Age of Reason*. Translated by Richard Howard, Vintage-Random House, 1988.

- If a source is listed as a certain edition or **version** of something, include that in your citation next.

- If a source is part of a **numbered** sequence, such as the magazine article listed under the title section above, that would be listed next.

- The **publisher** comes next in your citation.

- You do not need to include the publisher when you cite periodicals (magazines, newspapers, journals), works that are published by their author or editor, websites whose publishers share the name of the website, or websites that make works available but don't actually publish them (such as YouTube).

- The **publication date** is usually just a year. However, if the specific date is relevant to your paper, you'll want to cite that (when a TV show aired, for example).

- The **location** is where you found the specific information you're citing. It might be page numbers, web pages, etc.

In-text citations

- In-text citations are a short mention within the body of your paper that shows the source you got that particular information from. An in-text citation is usually just the author's name and page number in parentheses, or just the page number if you mention the author in the sentence.
  - After all, "you can't befriend someone and have a strong relationship if you aren't involved in his or her life" (Duckworth 25).

-or-

  - As Duckworth reminds us, "you can't befriend someone and have a strong relationship if you aren't involved in his or her life" (25).

-or-

  - It's hard to build a relationship with someone when you're not involved in their life (Duckworth 25).
  - Your Works Cited page would cite the full article:
    - Duckworth, Brittany Bartel. "Getting Along With Your Siblings." *Brio*, vol. 21, no. 3, 2017, pp. 24-25.

- If you are citing a work for which you don't know the author, use a shortened title of the work (in quotes if it's a short work, in italics if it's a longer work), and a page number if that's available.

- If you are citing a work that shares a last name with another source you're citing, use the author's first initials or full first names with their last name to differentiate.
  - (A. Johnson 12)

- For a work with more than one author, use both author's names with a page number.
  - (Smith and Eaton 173)

- For a work with more than two authors, simply use the first author's last name and replace the additional authors' names with et al.
  - (Maddox et al. 213)

- If you have more than one work by the same author, you'll want to denote which work you are referencing within your text. As before, use quotes for a short work like an article, and italics for a longer work like a book.
  - (Rivero, "It's a Conspiracy" 12)

  -or-

  - Rivero draws our attention to… ("It's a Conspiracy" 12)

- If you're citing the Bible in your paper, you'll want to make sure the first reference to the Bible makes clear which Bible you're using (underlined or italicized), followed by the book, chapter, and verse (not italicized or underlined).
  - Ezekiel saw "what seemed to be four living creatures," each with different faces, including that of a man, ox, lion, and eagle (*New Jerusalem Bible*, Ezek. 1.5-10).
    - Provided you're using the same Bible for future references, you can just use book, chapter, and verse in future citations within your paper.
      - There are echoes of this same imagery found in John's revelation written from the Isle of Patmos (Rev. 4.6-8).

- When citing sources of a digital nature, keep in mind that the point of all of these in-text citations is to point people to which source on your Works Cited page contains the information you are referencing. If they want to learn more or research further themselves, they know where to go. So using the first item that appears in the entry on your Works Cited page in the parentheses is the best way to handle these sources (author name, article name, website name, movie name, etc. Whatever appears first for that particular source on your Works Cited page).
  - URLs should only be included if that's the only way to differentiate what source you're referencing. Providing a partial URL is fine instead of the full web address (such as *money.com* versus http://www.money.com).

- If you're referencing more than one source in the same sentence, separate the citations by a semi-colon.
  - …as has been fully argued other places (Huey 17; Xander 32).

This lesson is by no means an exhaustive list. Full MLA manuals can be an inch or more thick. Hopefully this information covers most of what you would need, but you can always check online for guidance for your particular source or situation to be sure you're following the guidelines.

Lesson 3: Plagiarism

You should always cite your sources to avoid plagiarism. What is plagiarism?

- Plagiarism is stealing someone else's ideas and words and passing them off as your own.
    - U.S. law protects almost all forms of expression, as long as they are written or recorded in some manner. Copyright laws exist to protect original ideas.

    - The website "plagiarism.org" lists all of the following as acts of plagiarism:
        - turning in someone else's work as yours
        - copying words or ideas from someone without giving them credit
        - omitting quotation marks from a quotation
        - not giving correct information about a quote's source
        - changing words but copying the sentence structure without giving credit
        - copying so many words or ideas from someone else that it makes up the majority of your work (this is not okay even if you give credit).[1]

    - Plagiarism doesn't just apply to writing. Video, music, pictures, and other works of intellectual property that aren't original to you are all subject to plagiarism if you use them without attributing them. (Many YouTube or social media videos are taken down because they contain music that is copyrighted, for instance.)

    - Most instances of plagiarism can be avoided if you thoroughly cite your sources. We discussed how to do this in MLA style in Lesson 2.

- Take this plagiarism quiz. Record your score on your grading sheet.

1. Plagiarism can be avoided by thoroughly citing sources.   True   False

2. Ideas cannot really be stolen.   True   False

3. You can use a Works Cited list for listing the sources you've used.   True   False

4. If you paraphrase or summarize a document, you don't have to cite the source.   True   False

5. Sometimes something popular, like playing covers of copyrighted songs, can still be considered plagiarism.   True   False

---

[1] "What Is Plagiarism?" *Plagiarismorg RSS*, 18 May 2017, https://www.plagiarism.org/article/what-is-plagiarism.

Lesson 4: Evaluating Sources

Read about evaluating online sources for credibility.

- You can find anything you want to on the internet. Whether .com, .org, or any other extension, any opinion can be backed up by a website. It can be difficult to know what to believe when you're searching online. But there are questions you can ask and things you can look for to help you evaluate whether an online source is credible or not.

- **Author**
    o Can you find the name of the author on the page? Can you find their credentials?
    o What qualifies the author to write about the topic?
    o Is the parent page an organization or individual? Does the parent page lend credibility?
    o Does an internet search of the author's name bring up any helpful information?

- **Motive**
    o Does the site exist to inform? To persuade? To sell a product?
    o Who is the intended audience?

- **Impartiality**
    o Is the information fact or opinion?
    o Is the author biased in some way?
    o Is the language used free from emotion?

- **Accuracy**
    o Can you verify the information from other sources?
    o Is the information free of grammatical and spelling errors?
    o Are any sources cited? Can you assess their credibility?

- **Reliability**
    o Why should the information given be believed?
    o Does the information seem well-researched?
    o Is the site up-to-date? Do links on the site work?

- Some people use the CRAAP test (especially for online sources), developed by librarians at California State University, Chico:

    o **Current**
        ▪ Is it recent? Can you locate a date when it was created or updated?

    o **Reliable**
        ▪ Is the content mostly fact or opinion? Is the information biased? Do the authors provide references? Do the links work?

- Authority
  - Can you determine the author? Is there a way to contact them? Do they have credentials?

- Accuracy
  - Is the information supported by evidence? Can you verify the information on another reliable source? Are there errors on the page?

- Purpose
  - What's the goal of the website? Is it informative, persuasive, something else? Are there ads on the site? Is the writing style formal or informal?

Read over these ideas and when you're ready, take the quiz on the next page.

Lesson 4: Evaluating Sources Quiz

Take the following true/false quiz and record your score on your grade sheet.

1. To check authority of a website, you should look for the author/sponsor and contact information.

    True   False

2. All websites can be trusted as sources.

    True   False

3. Some of the most reliable website extensions include .com and .net.

    True   False

4. Bias is not important when evaluating the credibility of a website.

    True   False

5. If the author of the article cites sources, it's more likely to be accurate.

    True   False

Lesson 4: Evaluating Sources Rubric

You will reference this rubric to evaluate online sources as you do online research.

	Credible	Somewhat credible	Not very credible	Not at all credible
Accuracy	Information is reliable and can be verified by other reliable sources. There are no errors.	Information can be verified by most other reliable sources. There are few to no errors.	Information contains errors and is difficult to confirm.	Information is not accurate and conflicts with reliable sources.
Authors	Authors are listed and are reputable in the field. Contact information is available.	Authors are not listed but sponsors or the site of origin are easy to determine.	Author is not reputable in the field.	Author or sponsor information is not available.
Bias	The site is free of bias and alternate viewpoints are presented.	It's difficult to determine if the material is fact or opinion.	There are evidences of bias in the content.	The site is clearly biased, twisting words to fit an agenda.
Content	The content of the site is reliable, comes from primary sources, is consistent with what is already known, and is well-documented and supported with data.	Content is mostly supported by data and mostly consistent with what is already known. May or may not use primary sources.	Content is incomplete and inconsistent with what is already known and other reliable sources.	Content is inaccurate or suspect. Neither data nor sources are given.
Resources	A complete list of sources is given and the author clearly explains where they got their information.	Sources are referenced but there is not a complete list.	Sources are not referenced, but an incomplete list exists on the site.	The author doesn't mention anywhere what sources were used.
Timeliness	Links are current, content is updated, revision dates are displayed.	The content is mostly current for the topic.	Revision dates are old. There are broken or dead links.	No revision dates are given and links are expired.

As you read *The Adventures of Tom Sawyer*, you are going to be learning about writing a literary analysis. First, here are some of the technical parts of a literary analysis.

- The title of the work you are analyzing goes in italics if it is a play, novel, magazine, newspaper, or journal.
  - Mark Twain's *The Adventures of Tom Sawyer* is a classic novel.

- The title goes in quotes if it's a poem, short story, or article.
  - Emily Dickinson's poem "Fame is a Bee" is quick, but powerful.

- Your literary analysis should be double spaced.

- Anything in quotes should be exactly as it's written in the work you're quoting.
  - Remember that in the United States, periods and commas go inside the quotes, regardless of logic.
    - Jim was aptly described in chapter one as "getting into mischief."
    - The book aptly taught that "we all have a gift, but some are more obvious than others."
  - Other punctuation (question mark, exclamation point, semicolon, colon) goes wherever logic would say it goes.
    - For instance, if the quotation is a question, the question mark goes inside the quotation marks.
      - The book ended with a fitting question: "What do you think of that?"
    - But if the quotation is part of a broader question, the question mark would go outside the quotation marks.
      - Do you think we'll ever see "the land of a thousand suns"?

- Short quotations
  - In MLA formatting, short quotations include four typed lines or fewer of prose or three lines or fewer of verse.
  - If you're utilizing a short quotation in your text, enclose the quotation in double quotation marks and type it in line with the normal flow of your paper.

- Long quotations
  - Any quotations that include more than four lines of prose or three lines of verse do not need quotation marks. Instead, they are started on a new line, indented a half inch from the left margin (still double-spaced). For example:

In our study of Isaiah 6, we can't ignore this important tidbit at the beginning of the first verse:

> Our first verse says that this commissioning of Isaiah took place 'In the year that King Uzziah
>
> died.' A lot of times, Scripture passages don't really give us such a specific clue as to when

they happened. 'Later,' or 'When some time had passed,' or 'When he had grown old,' or other vague mentions of time are quite common throughout the Bible. But this passage is locked down into a very specific year – the year that King Uzziah died.

- In a literary analysis, it's generally regarded as okay to use the first person singular *I* that is often avoided in other written works. Some teachers and professors prefer what's known as the "journalistic we" (We learn about her illness in chapter two.) If you're able to write without using the first person at all, that's always preferred in formal essays and papers. Whatever you decide, be consistent throughout the paper.

- Your literary analysis should be written in the present tense in all cases where it makes sense to do so.
    - In the book, the author *calls* us to consider…
    - The main character *visits* her mother…
    - The language *implies*…
    - But then if you're writing about the history of the author, he *was born*… he *died*… these make more sense as past tense and are fine to write as such.
        - Biographical information isn't necessary unless it plays into the point of your analysis.
            - Because the author suffered with anxiety, we are drawn to the character's struggle with depression that much more.

- As with all other essays, your analysis will need an introduction, a thesis, and a conclusion.

Before you begin your actual paper, you will need to develop a thesis statement. (You will not be able to write your thesis until you have read part of or the entire novel.) You should already be familiar with what a thesis statement is. But here is a quick review.

- A thesis is the main idea of an essay. It should be stated in a complete sentence and include detail about what you plan to write about.

- A thesis statement is specific.
    - Rather than "There are many lessons presented in the novel."
    - It should be "The primary lesson presented in the novel is…"

- As you read through *The Adventures of Tom Sawyer*, you will be taking notes for questions or ideas that interest you. When you finish reading, you'll use your notes to come up with a question and answer that will help you form your thesis statement. I don't want to influence what you write about, so I'll be using one of Literature and Composition I's readings, *The Necklace* as I give examples.
    - When reading *The Necklace*, were you most interested in what the author was suggesting about living to impress others? Choose some theme or pattern of ideas and then convey it in the form of a question and answer.

- - Question: What does the author seem to be suggesting about living to impress others?
  - Answer: The author suggests that living to impress others is a vain endeavor that backfires in the end.

- Feel free to come up with more than one idea. Next flesh out your idea a little more.
  - Question: How does the author of *The Necklace* develop the idea that living to impress others is a vain endeavor that backfires in the end?
  - Answer: He strips Mathilde Loisel of everything she holds dear all because of a necklace she wears to impress others.

- Now take your fleshed-out question and answer and turn them around to form a statement.
  - By stripping Mathilde Loisel of everything she holds dear because of a necklace she wears to impress others, the author of *The Necklace* develops the idea that living to impress others is a vain idea that backfires in the end.

- Once you have a thesis statement, you'll need to show evidence to support your thesis.
  - In the above example, you'd need to show examples from the story that show the author stripping Mathilde Loisel of everything she holds dear and show how that develops the idea that living to impress others is a vain idea. You'd show how it backfires in the end.

Take the literary terms quiz on the next page to finish today's lesson.

Lesson 5: Literary Terms Quiz

Take this literary terms quiz and record your score on your grade sheet. This should be review.

1. Which term refers to the struggle in the story, usually between the protagonist and antagonist?

    a. setting   b. theme   c. conflict

2. The protagonist is _____ .

    a. the main/central character, sometimes called the hero
    b. the character who opposes the main character, typically creating the conflict
    c. the voice used to tell the story

3. The time and location in which the story takes place is the _____ .

    a. point of view   b. setting   c. theme

4. The antagonist is _____ .

    a. the main/central character, sometimes called the hero
    b. the character who opposes the main character, typically creating the conflict
    c. the voice used to tell the story

5. The theme of a novel is _____ .

    a. the struggle between characters
    b. the main idea; the point of the story
    c. the time and place in which the story takes place

Continue to learn about writing a literary analysis.

- Some potential topics for your paper might include:
  - Theme of your novel (meaning and evidence throughout the story)
  - Symbolism in the novel (instances and meanings)
  - Character analysis (motives of character, appearance, etc. and how they are all tied together and to the story)
  - Comparison/contrast between two character (protagonist/antagonist relationship)
  - Setting of your novel (how the author uses the setting to reach the reader and impact the plot)
  - Conflict in your novel (what is it, who is involved, what makes it important)
  - The history of your novel (why it is important to the story and how the author uses it)

- Novel Research Paper Requirements
  - Although you aren't going to begin writing right now, you will need to carefully review the requirements before you start. Here are the requirements:
    - Between 800 – 1100 words (2-3 pages)
    - Times New Roman or Arial font, 12 point, double spaced
    - MLA format (include correct page headings on all pages)
    - Must contain in-text citations, correctly formatted
    - Must contain at least five quotes/paraphrases: two from your novel and three from outside sources
    - Works Cited Page, correctly formatted
    - A minimum of five sources for your paper, including the novel. So you can count your novel as one source, and then find four more outside sources. You may have no more than three websites for your sources. Use books, journal articles, etc.

- Helpful hints for writing your paper
  - Take notes as you read your novel.
  - Write down important or interesting quotes with page numbers.
  - Write down interesting facts in your novel (setting, character actions, plot points, etc.).
  - Develop a potential thesis and look for information to support that as you read.
  - Look for outside sources as you read your novel. Keep a list of these (title, author, location, date, etc.).

- Tips and Reminders
  - Check sources for accuracy, authority, bias, timeliness, resources, and content.
  - Remember 1 inch margins all around, double space throughout, 12 point font.
  - You must cite your sources for direct quotes, paraphrases, and summaries. Use the general (author page) style, unless information is missing.
  - Use an alphabetical list of sources by author's last name. If there is no author, alphabetize by the title of the work.

o The first page of your paper needs the left aligned header: Name, Instructor, Course, Date (double spaced). All pages need the upper right hand corner heading with your last name and page number.

o Review plot, characters, setting, tone, symbols, theme, etc. Check out literary terms websites for more help.

o While your thesis statement presents your own viewpoint, it should not sound like a personal narrative.

o This is the guiding focus of your writing and is the center of your paper's meaning. Make it strong and to the point.

Lesson 6: Literary Analysis Rubric Lit & Comp II LA

This is the grading rubric you will use for your literary analysis. Keep it in mind as you prepare.

Content		
All information is factually correct 10	Most information is factually correct 9 - 4	Many factual errors/inconsistencies 3 - 1
Excellent background, context, and idea development 10	Adequate background, context, and idea development 9 - 4	Poor background, context, and idea development 3 - 1
Thesis is clear 10	Thesis is adequate 9 - 4	Thesis is poor 3 - 1
Excellent variety of sources 5	Adequate variety of sources 4 - 2	Inadequate variety of sources 1
Excellent discussion of detail 10	Adequate discussion of detail 9 - 4	Vague discussion of detail 3 - 1
Impressive depth of insight/analysis 10	Adequate depth of insight/analysis 9 - 4	Unexceptional insight/analysis 3 - 1
Effective conclusion/integration 10	Adequate conclusion/integration 9 – 4	Weak conclusion/integration 3 -1
Format and Style		
Excellent MLA style 5	Adequate MLA style 4-2	Poor MLA style 1
Clear organization 10	Adequate organization 9 - 4	Confusing organization 3 - 1
Smooth transitions 5	Adequate transitions 4 - 2	Awkward transitions 1
Correct grammar/no spelling mistakes 10	Few grammar errors/few spelling mistakes 9 - 4	Incorrect grammar/many spelling mistakes 3 - 1
Clean/legible manuscript 5	Adequate manuscript 4 – 2	Sloppy manuscript 1
Total Points:		(100 possible)

(Rubric adapted from GAVL, creative commons 3.0 [https://creativecommons.org/licenses/by/3.0/], cms.gavirtualschool.org/ Shared/ Language%20Arts/10thLitComp/01_NovelResearch/ResearchPaperGradingRubric.pdf)

Lesson 7: MLA Format Quiz

Go back to Lesson 1 and study the terms until you know them well enough to quiz yourself here. Then come back to this page and fill in the definitions for each.

Thesis Statement: _____

_____

_____

Topic Sentence: _____

_____

Introduction Paragraph: _____

_____

_____

Body Paragraph: _____

_____

_____

_____

Conclusion Paragraph: _____

_____

_____

_____

(continued on next page)

Development Sentence: _____

_____

_____

Evidence: _____

_____

_____

Analysis Sentence: _____

_____

_____

Conclusion Sentence: _____

_____

_____

In-Text Citation: _____

_____

_____

Source Citation: _____

_____

_____

Works Cited: _____

_____

Remember that each complete sentence has three parts: a subject (who or what the sentence is about), a predicate (the verb or action), and it is a complete thought (it can stand alone and make sense).

- Some sentences can be complete, though very short.
  - We stopped.
    - This sentence has a subject (we) and predicate (stopped). It is also a complete thought and can stand alone.
- Some sentences are complete and much longer.
  - We stopped when the light turned red.
  - We stopped when the light turned red while we were on our way to the bank.
  - Wishing we had left a little earlier so we wouldn't miss our appointment, we stopped when the light turned red while we were on our way to the bank.

- A **sentence fragment** is an incomplete sentence.
  - A fragment can be incomplete because it is lacking a subject, verb, or both.
  - More often, a sentence is a fragment because it does not express a complete thought.
    - While we were on our way to the bank (what happened?)
    - Wishing we had left a little earlier (why were we wishing that?)
    - When the light turned red (what then?)
      - Each of these has a subject and verb. But they are still fragments because they do not express a complete thought.

- **Subordinating conjunctions** are words that join two sentences together, making one of the sentences dependent on the other for a complete thought.
  - Subordinating conjunctions do not have to be at the beginning of the sentence.
    - When the light turned red, we stopped.
    - We stopped when the light turned red.
      - What's the subordinating conjunction? Here it's the word *when*.
        - We stopped.
        - The light turned red.
          - Both of these are complete sentences. By joining them together with the word *when*, we turn *when the light turned red* into a dependent clause that must be joined to *We stopped* to form a complete thought.

- **Run-on sentences** occur when two complete sentences are put together without proper separation.
  - My favorite sport is soccer it is very easy to learn.
    - This is two complete sentences shoved together without punctuation.
  - There are several ways to correct run-on sentences.
    - You can use a semicolon:
      - My favorite sport is soccer; it is very easy to learn.

- You can use a comma with a coordinating conjunction (remember FANBOYS, for, and, nor, but, or, yet, so):
  - My favorite sport is soccer, and it is very easy to learn.
  - My favorite sport is soccer, for it is very easy to learn.
- You can use a period to separate the two sentences.
  - My favorite sport is soccer. It is very easy to learn.
- You can use a subordinating conjunction:
  - My favorite sport is soccer because it is very easy to learn.
  - Because it is very easy to learn, my favorite sport is soccer.
- You can use an em dash (or long dash) to emphasize the second sentence:
  - My favorite sport is soccer – it is very easy to learn.
- **Special tips**: to help find run-ons, you can try these two tests:
  - Turn your sentence into a yes or no question.
  - Turn your sentence into a tag question.
    - My favorite sport is soccer.
      - Is my favorite sport soccer?
      - My favorite sport is soccer, isn't it?
        - Both tests work, so this sentence is not a run-on.
    - My favorite sport is soccer it is very easy to learn.
      - Is my favorite sport soccer it is very easy to learn?
      - My favorite sport is soccer it is very easy to learn, isn't it?
        - The tests don't work. This must be a run-on.
          - Note that in this example, the first test is easier to spot as an error. But if you look closely, you're really asking two questions in the second test as well.
            - My favorite sport is soccer, isn't it?
            - It is very easy to learn, isn't it?

- Do NOT fix a run-on by simply adding a comma between the two sentences. This creates a **comma splice**.
  - My favorite sport is soccer, it is very easy to learn.
    - A comma splice is fixed the same way a run-on sentence is: change the punctuation or add a conjunction of some kind.

- If you need to review any information, do so. Then take the quiz on the next page.

Identify whether each group of words is a run-on, complete sentence, or fragment. Check your answers and learn from any mistakes.

1. Which was created in 1979.
   a. run-on   b. complete sentence   c. fragment

2. She needed the ingredients for cookies, she went to the store.
   a. run-on   b. complete sentence   c. fragment

3. Needed the materials for the science project.
   a. run-on   b. complete sentence   c. fragment

4. Lee Giles created Easy Peasy curriculum and Genesis Curriculum.
   a. run-on   b. complete sentence   c. fragment

5. We have too much homework, we have no time for fun.
   a. run-on   b. complete sentence   c. fragment

6. When we have to stay up too late.
   a. run-on   b. complete sentence   c. fragment

7. The dog chewed up the shoes, he made a huge mess.
   a. run-on   b. complete sentence   c. fragment

8. Reading is a great way to pass the time.
   a. run-on   b. complete sentence   c. fragment

9. After I spilled taco seasoning everywhere.
   a. run-on   b. complete sentence   c. fragment

10. Compared to all the other bakers, she makes the best cake.
    a. run-on   b. complete sentence   c. fragment

Read these poetic terms and definitions. Use them to complete the crossword puzzle on the next page.

alliteration: the repetition of words that have the same first consonant sounds next to or close to each other (She sells seashells by the seashore.)

allusion: an indirect reference to something such as another work of literature, a historical event, biblical story, mythical character, etc. (a Herculean effort; open Pandora's Box)

blank verse: un-rhyming verse written in iambic pentameter ("To sleep – perchance to dream: ay, there's the rub!")

consonance: repetitive sounds produced by consonants within a sentence or phrase (Toss the grass, boss.)

descriptive essay: an essay that uses similes, metaphors, and other figurative language to illustrate something in a way the reader can see, feel, or hear what is being written

feet: the combination of stressed and unstressed syllables

figurative language: uses figures of speech to be more effective, persuasive, and impactful

hyperbole: a figure of speech that is an extreme exaggeration in order to create emphasis (I'm so hungry, I could eat a horse.)

iambic pentameter: an iamb is a type of foot consisting of one stressed syllable and one unstressed syllable (such as the word "remark"). "Pent" means five. So a line of iambic pentameter consists of five iambs – five sets of unstressed syllables followed by stressed syllables. ("To be, or not to be, that is the question.")

metaphor: a figure of speech that makes a direct comparison and shows similarities between two different things without using "like" or "as" (My sister is a bear if she doesn't get enough sleep.)

meter: a unit of rhythm in poetry; the pattern of the beats. It is also called a foot. Each foot has a certain number of syllables in it, usually two or three syllables. The difference in types of meter is which syllables are accented and which are not.

oxymoron: a figure of speech in which two opposite ideas are joined to create an effect ("parting is such sweet sorrow")

personification: a figure of speech in which a thing, an idea, or an animal is given human attributes (The wind howled through the night.)

repetition: a literary device that repeats the same words or phrases a few times to make an idea clearer ("It was the best of times, it was the worst of times.")

rhyme: two or more words or phrases that end in the same sound

Shakespearean sonnet: the sonnet form used by Shakespeare, composed of three quatrains and a terminal couplet in iambic pentameter with the rhyme pattern abab cdcd efef gg

> Shall I compare thee to a summer's day?
> Thou art more lovely and more temperate:
> Rough winds do shake the darling buds of May,
> And summer's lease hath all too short a date;
> Sometime too hot the eye of heaven shines,
> And often is his gold complexion dimm'd;
> And every fair from fair sometime declines,
> By chance or nature's changing course untrimm'd;
> But thy eternal summer shall not fade,
> Nor lose possession of that fair thou ow'st;
> Nor shall death brag thou wander'st in his shade,
> When in eternal lines to time thou grow'st:
>> So long as men can breathe or eyes can see,
>> So long lives this, and this gives life to thee.

simile: a figure of speech that makes a comparison and shows similarities between two different things by using "like" or "as" (Life is like a box of chocolates.)

sonnet: a poem of fourteen lines using any number of formal rhyme schemes; in English – typically having ten syllables per line

stanza: a group of lines in a poem

symbol: an object or idea that represents or stands for something else – especially a material object having a deeper meaning (the One Ring in *Lord of the Rings*)

Complete the crossword puzzle.

Across:

3. a group of lines in a poem, like paragraphs in an essay
5. repetition of the same sounds in words
8. the repetition of initial sounds in neighboring words
9. the recurrence of the same words, lines, or stanzas to enhance the mood

Down:

1. a direct comparison between two unlike things without using "like" or "as"
2. an extreme exaggeration used to make a point
4. a comparison between two unlike things using "like" or "as"
6. when something concrete stands for something that is abstract
7. a reference to another person, place, event, or literary work/character

Lesson 9: Poetic Devices

Read "The Road Not Taken," by Robert Frost. What is the rhyme scheme? What figurative language or poetic devices are used? What literary elements can you find? Use line numbers to indicate where you find them.

1	Two roads diverged in a yellow wood,
2	And sorry I could not travel both
3	And be one traveler, long I stood
4	And looked down one as far as I could
5	To where it bent in the undergrowth;
6	Then took the other, as just as fair,
7	And having perhaps the better claim,
8	Because it was grassy and wanted wear;
9	Though as for that the passing there
10	Had worn them really about the same,
11	And both that morning equally lay
12	In leaves no step had trodden black.
13	Oh, I kept the first for another day!
14	Yet knowing how way leads on to way,
15	I doubted if I should ever come back.
16	I shall be telling this with a sigh
17	Somewhere ages and ages hence:
18	Two roads diverged in a wood, and I—
19	I took the one less traveled by,
20	And that has made all the difference.

_____

_____

_____

_____

_____

_____

(A nice reference for poetic devices can be found at chaparralpoets.org/devices.pdf if you need more in-depth study.)

Read these poems and the notes that accompany them.

Autumn
By T.E. Hulme

A touch of cold in the Autumn night—

I walked abroad,

And saw the ruddy moon lean over a hedge

Like a red-faced farmer.

I did not stop to speak, but nodded,

And round about were the wistful stars

With white faces like town children.

personification – the moon has the human ability to lean like a farmer
simile – comparing the moon to a farmer using "like"
alliteration – repetition of beginning sounds in neighboring words "stop" and "speak"
alliteration – repetition of beginning sounds in neighboring words "were," "wistful," "with," and "white"
simile – comparing the stars faces to those of town children using "like"

Fame is a fickle food
By Emily Dickinson

Fame is a fickle food

Upon a shifting plate

Whose table once a

Guest but not

The second time is set

Whose crumbs the crows inspect

And with ironic caw

Flap past it to the

Farmer's corn

Men eat of it and die

metaphor – fame is compared to a food without using "like" or "as" alliteration – repeating beginning "f" sound
consonance – repeating "t" sound in table, guest, not, time, set (even the word "second" when read right before "time" seems to end with the "t" sound.)
alliteration – repeating beginning hard "c"
consonance – repeating hard "c" in "ironic" and "caw"
consonance – repeating "p" sound in "flap" and "past"
hyperbole – using the extreme of "death" to explain how fame affects people

Lesson 10: Analyzing Poetry

Now read this poem and answer the questions that follow it.

A Red, Red Rose
by Robert Burns

I.
O, my luve's like a red, red rose,
That's newly sprung in June:
O, my luve's like the melodie,
That's sweetly play'd in tune.

II.
As fair art thou, my bonnie lass,
So deep in luve am I:
And I will luve thee still, my dear,
'Till a' the seas gang dry.

III.
'Till a' the seas gang dry, my dear,
And the rocks melt wi' the sun:
I will luve thee still, my dear,
While the sands o' life shall run.

IV.
And fare thee weel, my only luve!
And fare thee weel a-while!
And I will come again, my luve,
Tho' it were ten thousand mile.

Which line is an example of simile?
a. "And I will come again, my luve"
b. "O, my luve's like a red, red rose"
c. "And the rocks melt wi' the sun"

Another example of simile is:
a. "So deep in luve am I"
b. "I will luve thee still, my dear"
c. "O, my luve's like the melodie"

In the third stanza, lines 2 and 4 are examples of:
a. simile   b. rhyme   c. repetition

In the fourth stanza, the beginning of lines 1 and 2 are an example of:
a. repetition   b. hyperbole   c. simile

Lesson 11: Imitating Poetic Devices

Read over and complete this poetic devices assignment.

Step 1
Choose a poem we read in this course, or any other poem.

Step 2
Read and study the poem, making a list of poetic devices found in the poem.

Step 3
Then, write your own poem using the poetic devices from the original poem. For instance, if the poem contains alliteration, simile, and hyperbole, your new poem should include those devices. You can imitate the entire poem, rewriting the words, or you can write your own using the same devices.

If you need an example, you can check the online course. The link in #1 contains an example.

(Assignment from GAVL, creative commons 3.0 [https://creativecommons.org/licenses/by/3.0/], http://cms.gavirtualschool.org/Shared/ Language%20Arts/10thLitComp/02_PoetryOne/index.html)

Here's the rubric for your assignment. Record your score on your grading sheet.

5 points maximum for each area, 25 total points possible for assignment

1. Student followed assignment directions and wrote poem
2. Student correctly identified poetic devices in original poem
3. Student correctly used same poetic devices in new poem
4. Student uses correct grammar and spelling throughout
5. Student understands overall meaning of poem

(Rubric adapted from GAVL, creative commons 3.0 [https://creativecommons.org/licenses/by/3.0/], http://cms.gavirtualschool.org/Shared/ Language%20Arts/10thLitComp/02_PoetryOne/ShelSilverstein_ImitatingPoeticDevices_AssignmentRubric.pdf)

Identify whether each group of words is a run-on, complete sentence, or fragment. If it is a run-on or fragment, correct the error.

1. While I was going to the library Friday.

2. We had lasagna for dinner last night it was delicious.

3. She jumped.

4. After going to the park, Michal was tired.

5. Because no one told her to bring her paint clothes.

6. Since Ezra switched school districts.

7. Rachel brought her spaghetti to the table, she spilled it all over the chair.

8. The kids ran through the rain, and then they got water all over the floor.

9. Believing that tomorrow would be a better day.

10. Whenever the snowstorm ends.

11. Give three ways to fix a run-on sentence:

_____

_____

_____

Lesson 12: Sentence Quiz

What choice best describes the group of words presented?

1. I like apples, she likes bananas, he likes oranges.
    a. run-on   b. complete sentence   c. fragment

2. With all this rain, my yard is going to flood soon.
    a. run-on   b. complete sentence   c. fragment

3. I went to the movies, I went to the store.
    a. run-on   b. complete sentence   c. fragment

4. After the biggest earthquake I've ever experienced in my life.
    a. run-on   b. complete sentence   c. fragment

5. We should go to the store because we are out of bread.
    a. run-on   b. complete sentence   c. fragment

6. My dog ran away, but then he came back.
    a. run-on   b. complete sentence   c. fragment

7. When you write with a pen with blue ink and it smudges.
    a. run-on   b. complete sentence   c. fragment

8. We exercised all week, we prepared for the track meet.
    a. run-on   b. complete sentence   c. fragment

9. The winter catalogue had a sale on sweaters, boots, and scarves.
    a. run-on   b. complete sentence   c. fragment

10. All my dirty laundry.
    a. run-on   b. complete sentence   c. fragment

Lesson 13: Poetic Devices

Choose which poetic/literary device is represented in each example.

1. She sells sea shells by the seashore.

    a. consonance   b. assonance   c. alliteration   d. oxymoron

2. The BOOM of the fireworks shook the windows.

    a. simile   b. onomatopoeia   c. metaphor   d. personification

3. My mom tells me to clean by room a thousand times a day.

    a. hyperbole   b. allusion   c. simile   d. metaphor

4. The tree was a fortress, protecting our picnic from the rain.

    a. consonance   b. metaphor   c. alliteration   d. simile

5. The black cat attacked the wrapping paper.

    a. allusion   b. assonance   c. alliteration   d. repetition

6. The clouds were like fluffy cotton candy.

    a. metaphor   b. onomatopoeia   c. oxymoron   d. simile

7. He lifted the couch with Herculean strength.

    a. allusion   b. consonance   c. cliché   d. metaphor

8. The wind whispered through the leaves.

    a. hyperbole   b. assonance   c. personification   d. repetition

9. We must, we MUST get there in time!

    a. repetition   b. hyperbole   c. metaphor   d. simile

10. It's the same difference.

    a. onomatopoeia   b. alliteration   c. oxymoron   d. allusion

Lesson 14: Analyzing Poetry Project

For the next three lessons you will be completing a project analyzing poetry. You will choose a poet and analyze two poems, creating a presentation about the poet and the chosen works. Here are the directions you will follow for the project:

- Step 1: Choose a poet to research from the list below
  - Rita Dove
  - Emily Dickinson
  - Nikki Giovanni
  - Seamus Heaney
  - Langston Hughes
  - William Carlos Williams
  - Edwin Arlington Robinson
  - Countee Cullen
  - William Wordsworth
  - Ralph Waldo Emerson
  - Amy Lowell
  - Dorothy Parker

- Step 2: Choose two poems by that poet to read and analyze

- Step 3: Create a multimedia presentation that displays the information.
  - Multimedia presentations can be in PowerPoint, Sway, or other program similar to those.
    - Presentation components should include (each number is a slide):
      - 1 – title page
      - 2 – poet name and picture(s) with citations
      - 3 – 8-10 poet facts
      - 4 – Poem 1 text
      - 5-6 – Poem 1 analysis
      - 7 – Poem 2 text
      - 8-9 – Poem 2 analysis
      - 10 – Works cited page

- Poem Analysis Requirements:
  - Identify poetic devices in poem
  - Explain the significance of the devices (how they enhance or contribute to the poem)
  - Give a 2 – 4 sentence summary of the poem's overall meaning

** Remember to cite any information you use throughout the presentation. Citations should be found on the slide/page in which they occur.

Lesson 14: Analyzing Poetry Rubric

Read over the grading rubric to make sure you do what it takes to get a perfect score:

Slide 1 – Title page (5 points)

Slide 2 – Poet name and picture(s) with citations (5 points)

Slide 3 – 8-10 poet facts (10 points)

Slide 4 – Poem 1 text (10 points)
- poem is readable and title is shown

Slides 5-6 – Poem 1 analysis (15 points)
- all poetic devices are identified
- poetic devices are explained correctly

Slide 7 – Poem 2 text (10 points)
- poem is readable and title is shown

Slides 8-9 – Poem 2 analysis (15 points)
- all poetic devices are identified
- poetic devices are explained correctly

Slide 10 – Works Cited page (15 points)
- correctly formatted entries
- correct information and sources given

Overall (15 points)
- correct spelling, grammar, and punctuation used throughout

100 total points possible

(Rubric adapted from GAVL, creative commons 3.0 [https://creativecommons.org/licenses/by/3.0/], http://cms.gavirtualschool.org/Shared/Language%20Arts/10thLitComp/02_PoetryOne/AnalyzingPoetryProjectRubric.pdf)

You may ask a parent if you have a different idea for the form of your project, such as a movie, a poster, etc.

Lesson 15: Symbolism • Poetry Project Lit & Comp II LA

Continue to work on your analyzing poetry project. Make sure you are following all the directions and aiming for a perfect score. You need to finish on Lesson 16.

Here's a quick reminder about **symbolism**. Symbolism is when a person, place, or object represents an abstract idea beyond its literal meaning. It's used often in literature, theater, and cinema, but can also be found in everyday life very easily. Think of companies such as Apple or Nike that can be recognized with nothing but an image (a bitten apple or a swoosh). Sports teams are recognized by their logos. The various flags of the world are made up of symbols (such as the thirteen red and white stripes on the American flag symbolizing the thirteen original colonies and the fifty stars representing the fifty states).

Authors use symbolism to tie simple things to more universal themes. Symbolism is used across all types of literature and is not specific to any particular genre. Many literary devices (such as metaphor, allegory, and allusion) can be types of symbolism. Some well-known examples of symbolism in literature include Aslan in *The Lion, the Witch, and the Wardrobe* who symbolizes Jesus Christ, the scarlet letter in *The Scarlet Letter* that symbolizes sin, and the One Ring in *The Lord of the Rings* that symbolizes ultimate power. Shakespeare's writing is full of symbolism, such as using flowers as symbols for beauty and weeds as symbols for ugliness.

Symbolism is used in writing for many reasons. Some authors use it simply to be creative. Writing comes across as more poetic when it's full of symbolism. It can be more enjoyable and engaging for a reader to deduce the meaning of something through symbolism. Symbols are also a good way to make a complex concept more simple and relatable to the reader.

Think of ways you can use symbolism in your writing where it will serve you well.

Lesson 16: Analyzing Poetry Project Lit & Comp II LA

Finish and present your final poetry project. Use the grading rubric to score your project and record it on your grading sheet.

Lesson 17: Literary Analysis • Archetypes

Look back to Lesson 6 at your literary analysis assignment. Refresh your mind on what you're looking to accomplish with that assignment. You should have a topic in mind or at least have it narrowed down. Make sure you are taking notes with page references and quotes that support your topic and, if you have it planned, your thesis.

Now we're going to learn about archetypes in literature. An archetype is a repeated symbol or motif. The ones we'll discuss here are common, but of course, they're not always functioning as archetypes each time they appear in literature. You'll always want to use the context of what you're reading to determine if these images are being used as symbols. There are also obviously archetypes that aren't included here. These are just examples.

- Water
  - Water is possibly the most common archetype in literature. It can represent creation, rebirth, cleansing, and even the unconscious or a dream state.

- Sun
  - The sun (or sky or fire) often represents birth, creation, or a dawning of understanding (rising sun) or death (setting sun).

- Colors
  - Black
    - Black is generally a negative color and represents chaos, evil, death, and the unknown.
  - Blue
    - Blue is a positive color that is often associated with truth and security.
  - Green
    - Green tends to represent growth and hope.
  - Red
    - Red tends to be violent: blood, passion, sacrifice. It can also represent disorder.
  - White
    - White can be positive or negative. When positive, it represents purity and innocence. When negative, it represents death and fear/dread.

- Circles
  - Circles signify wholeness or unity.

- Snakes
  - Snakes generally signify evil, deceit, or corruption.

- Deserts
  - Deserts represent hopelessness and death.

- Garden
  - Gardens are often juxtaposed with deserts and represent paradise, fertility, and life.

- Motifs
  - There are many motifs in literature that are archetypal. The most popular is probably the hero.
    - The hero has some type of quest where he is faced with impossible tasks that he somehow overcomes. We'll read *The Odyssey* this year which will be a perfect example of this motif. *Idylls of the King* and *LeMorte D'Arthur* will feature King Arthur, another stereotypical literary hero.

- Genres
  - Seasons can function as archetypal genres.
    - Winter – irony
    - Spring – comedy
    - Summer – romance
    - Fall - tragedy

- Verbs have two "voices" – active and passive.
  - In the **active** voice, the subject does the action.
    - The youth group washed the cars.
  - In the **passive** voice, the subject is receiving the action.
    - The cars were washed by the youth group.

- In writing, it is generally preferred that you use the active voice if you can. It tends to make the writing more interesting. But there are situations in which the passive voice is useful.

- Sometimes the passive voice is used in a protective, pass-the-buck sort of way.
  - "The corporate office informed the store that there was a misprint in the ad" puts responsibility on the corporate office while using the passive "The store was informed that there was a misprint in the ad" passes the buck.
  - In the same way, if you don't want to blame anyone in particular, you would use the passive voice.
    - I was given the wrong directions.

- The passive voice is useful when the doer of the action is unknown.
  - The garage door was left open.
    - You don't know who left it open.

- The passive voice is useful when the doer of the action is less important than the receiver of the action.
  - The package was delivered last week.
    - It doesn't matter who brought the package.
  - This is often the case in scientific or mechanical processes where the details are much more important than the person who is doing the action.
    - "Thirty cc of water was added to the solution" would be preferred in a lab report to "I added thirty cc of water to the solution."

Here are the passive forms of "purchase." (Passive forms of verbs are created by combining a form of the "to be" verb with the past participle of the main verb.)

Tense	Subject	Singular	Plural	Past Participle
Present	The gift/gifts	is	are	purchased.
Present perfect	The gift/gifts	has been	have been	purchased.
Past	The gift/gifts	was	were	purchased.
Past perfect	The gift/gifts	had been		purchased.
Future	The gift/gifts	will be		purchased.
Future perfect	The gift/gifts	will have been		purchased.
Present progressive	The gift/gifts	is being	are being	purchased.
Past progressive	The gift/gifts	was being	were being	purchased.

Lesson 19: Passive Voice

Learn more about the passive voice.

- To review, in the passive voice, the subject is receiving the action in the sentence.
  - To find a passive construct, look for a form of "to be" followed by a past participle.
    - See the chart in Lesson 18 to help with this.

- Some reasons passive voice is not generally preferred:
  - Passive voice can omit the actor from the sentence, therefore omitting clarity or meaning.
    - Passive: The city has been devastated. – Why? How? By whom or what?
      - Active: The tornado devastated the city.
    - Passive: Food was supplied to the victims.
      - Active: The American Red Cross supplied food to the victims.

  - Passive voice can expresses laziness in research.
    - Passive: African Americans were not treated as equals.
      - The reader doesn't learn anything about the conditions or human decisions that produced this oppression. No one is blamed or called out. There is no actor in this sentence. The reader doesn't even know if the author of the paper knows the answer to how, why, by whom. There is no depth of research expressed.

- When passive voice might be preferred or used:
  - Passive voice is preferred if you want to emphasize an object.
    - Passive: Thirteen civilians were killed in the bomb explosion.
      - The civilian deaths are more important than the unknown bomber.
    - Active: Someone killed thirteen civilians in the bomb explosion.
      - The active voice puts the emphasis on the wrong thing.

  - The passive voice is used to de-emphasize an unknown subject or actor.
    - My car was stolen.
      - I don't know who stole my car.
    - The lights were left on.
      - I don't know who left the lights on.

  - The passive voice is used if your readers don't need to know who's doing the action.
    - $150,000 was raised for the orphanage.
      - The donor possibly doesn't want to be recognized or emphasized.

  - The passive voice can be used to state facts or report things.
    - Interstate 40 was closed yesterday due to an overturned semi-truck.
    - A lot of rice is grown in China.
    - The baby giraffe was delivered overnight.

- If it's not helpful to the clarity of your writing, it's generally preferred that you reword passive voice into active voice.
  - To do this, you usually just need to rearrange the words to where the actor and the subject are the same word.
    - The city has been devastated by the tornado. (passive) "The city" is the subject while "the tornado" is the one doing the action.
    - The tornado devastated the city. (active) "The tornado" is both the subject and the actor.

- Pinning thoughts on the author or person you're researching can help you avoid the passive voice in some cases.
  - For instance, as you're writing your literary analysis, you can use this tactic:
    - Instead of "It is mentioned that..." you can say "Twain mentions that..."
    - Instead of "Tom and Huck are portrayed as..." you can say "Twain portrays Tom and Huck as..."

Write five sentences in the passive voice and then rewrite them without it.

_____

_____

_____

_____

_____

_____

_____

_____

_____

_____

_____

_____

Lesson 20: Passive Voice

Rewrite the following sentences to change the voice from passive to active. NOTE: not all of the sentences are in passive voice. Pay attention!

Flight of Her Life was written by Jennifer Appel.

_____

I was amazed by the weatherman's lack of accuracy.

_____

A surprise thunderstorm soaked us as we finished up our hike.

_____

Late last night, I was told the shocking news by my son.

_____

With three weeks to go in the semester, we were informed of a huge new assignment by our professor.

_____

_____

The hockey puck was fired off the glass by the defenseman.

_____

Lesson 21: Active and Passive Voice

Determine whether each sentence is in the active or the passive voice.

1. The two girls sometimes draw pictures.
                active   passive

2. The stereos are made in China.
                active   passive

3. Many trees were damaged by the hurricane.
                active   passive

4. Mr. Dossett conducted the band.
                active   passive

5. Bryce was riding his bike.
                active   passive

6. The Olympian ran the 100-yard dash.
                active   passive

7. Walls have been demolished.
                active   passive

8. The Dead Sea Scrolls are written in Hebrew.
                active   passive

9. You should have come with us.
                active   passive

10. The clothes were bought on sale.
                active   passive

Below are some ideas for the literary analysis you are going to write on *Tom Sawyer*. Be thinking about a topic and what examples you could use from the book. These ideas are adapted from the GAVL course cited previously.

- o Compare and contrast two characters
  - Consider a protagonist/antagonist relationship

- o Discuss a running theme throughout the novel
  - Consider meaning and evidence throughout the story

- o Discuss symbolism/imagery within the novel
  - Cite instances and meanings

- o Discuss how suspense, irony, or foreshadowing play a part in the novel
  - Cite examples and meanings

- o Connections to history in the novel
  - Why it is important to the story and how the author uses it.

- o Character analysis
  - motives of character, appearance, etc. and how they are all tied together and to the story

- o Setting of your novel
  - how the author uses the setting to reach the reader and impact the plot

- o Conflict in your novel
  - what is it, who is involved, what makes it important

You should be zeroing in on your topic if you haven't already. Your paper will be due by Lesson 31. We'll have one more in-depth lesson about literary analysis in Lesson 26.

The purpose of a literary analysis is to show a depth of understanding of the piece you're analyzing. Your analysis will be stronger if you utilize quotations and examples from the text.

- How to analyze
    - Have specific questions in mind as you're reading.
    - Identify the author's purpose. Why was the book written?
    - Examine your own personal reaction to the book and explore the depths of that reaction.
    - Think of all the elements of the story – characters, setting, plot, imagery. How do these elements enforce what the author is trying to do? How do they relate to the overall theme of the book?
    - Ascertain the most important ideas of the book and break them down.
    - Come up with a thesis or topic sentence that states the idea you'll be focusing on.

- How to utilize particular passages or quotations
    - Offer some context for the passage or quotation without flipping into "book report" mode. (Don't summarize too much.)
    - Cite the passage or quotation using the correct MLA format required for the paper.
    - Then describe how the passage or quotation fits your thesis or overall paper. Why is what you've quoted significant? What ideas are expressed? What language is used?
    - Repeat this process, offering context, citing the passage, describing how it's important, always working to support your thesis or topic sentence.

- Flip back to Lesson 6 to refresh yourself on the requirements of your paper. (You can use the word count feature in your word processing program to get the proper length.) Review the grading rubric to understand what is expected. Your paper is due by Lesson 31.

- If you need to see an example, you can find sample literary analysis papers linked in the online course in Lesson 26.

Lesson 27: Literary Analysis

Continue to work on your literary analysis. It's due on Lesson 31.

Lesson 28: Literary Analysis

Continue to work on your literary analysis. It's due on Lesson 31.

Lesson 29: Literary Analysis

Continue to work on your literary analysis. Refer to Lesson 6 for the assignment. Quote the text. Use examples. It's due on Lesson 31.

Lesson 30: Literary Analysis

Finish writing your literary analysis. Refer to Lesson 6 for the assignment. Quote the text. Use examples.

In Lesson 31 you will be grading your analysis and moving on to the next topic. Don't call it done just because you finished writing. Read it over and edit.

Finish your literary analysis. Grade your assignment based on the grading rubric from Lesson 6. Record your score on your grading sheet.

Hopefully this short story sequence depiction looks a little familiar:

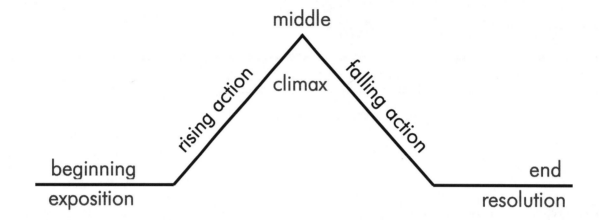

Except it should really look more like this next one. The climax isn't usually in the middle. The following diagram also shows that the story doesn't end in the same place it began. It shows the all-important initiating event: the something that happens that sets the plot in motion and raises the question that the story is going to answer.

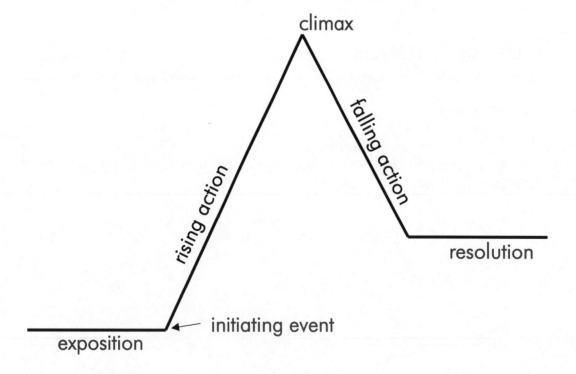

Read through this short story terminology. Then cover up the definitions and see how many you remember. Review the ones you have trouble with. Hopefully you're already familiar with most of them.

plot: the sequence of events in a story

setting: the time and place where a story takes place

exposition: the beginning of a story that introduces the characters, setting, and basis of the plot

conflict: a problem between a character and another person or force

internal conflict: a struggle inside a character's mind

external conflict: a struggle between a character and someone or something outside of the character

climax: the turning point in a story

rising action: events leading up to the climax

falling action: events following the climax that lead to the resolution

resolution: the end of a story where the conflict is solved or the outcome of the conflict is seen

character: a person (or an animal) in a literary work

characterization: the process of revealing the personality of a character

direct characterization: when the reader knows directly what a character's personality is like

indirect characterization: when a character's personality is revealed through actions or hints rather than directly

dynamic character: a changing character – one who grows and learns as the story goes on

flat character: a character the reader doesn't know very well or that isn't very developed

static character: a character that remains steady and does not change throughout the story

round character: a fully-developed character about whom the reader knows much

protagonist: the main character

antagonist: the character who works against the protagonist; often the "bad guy" or source of conflict

irony: a literary technique that portrays differences between what is said and what is meant (verbal), between what is seen and what is real (dramatic), and between what is expected and what actually happens (situational)

verbal irony: often portrayed as sarcasm, in this type of irony, what is said is opposite of what is meant

dramatic irony: type of irony in which facts or events are hidden from a character but known to the reader, audience, and/or other characters

situational irony: when what happens is very different from what was expected (a fire station burns down, for example)

theme: the main idea or meaning of a text

narrator: the person or character who tells the story

point of view: the perspective from which a story is told

1st Person Point of View: the narrator is a character in the story; uses words like I, me, my, we, our

3rd Person Limited Point of View: the narrator uses pronouns like "he," "she, and "it" to convey the thoughts and feelings of one character only

3rd Person Omniscient Point of View: the narrator knows the thoughts and feelings of every character; still uses pronouns "he," "she," and "it"

fiction: a story that is made up

nonfiction: writing about real people, places, or events

figurative language: language that uses figures of speech and can't be taken literally

genre: a category of literature characterized by content or a particular form or style (also applies to art, music, etc.)

imagery: descriptive language that appeals to the five senses

symbol: something that stands for something else

suspense: angst or uncertainty the reader feels about what is going to happen next

foreshadowing: hints and clues that suggest what will happen later in the story

Let's refresh our memories about irony.

- There are three main types of literary irony. These forms of irony are great tools for a writer to improve their story.
  - **Verbal irony** is a statement in which the meaning that a speaker uses is sharply different from the meaning that is seemingly portrayed.
    - Examples of verbal irony, often expressed as sarcasm:
      - Listening to a very long-winded speech and saying when it finally ends (while rolling your eyes), "Well *that* was short and sweet, wasn't it?"
      - Sitting in a traffic jam and exclaiming, "This will really help us make our connections in a timely manner today."
      - Being frustrated about an app locking up on your phone and stating, "Ugh! I'm going to throw my phone out the window!"

  - **Situational irony** is when the result of an action is the opposite of the desired or expected effect.
    - Examples of situational irony:
      - A fire station burning down.
      - Looking everywhere for your glasses when they're on your head.
      - Oversleeping and rushing to get ready, only to realize it's the weekend.

  - **Dramatic irony** is when words or actions hold a significance that the listener or audience understands, but the speaker or character does not.
    - Here are some well-known examples of dramatic irony:
      - *Romeo and Juliet* might have the most famous examples of dramatic irony (you'll be reading this play in a few weeks). In the play, the most popular example of dramatic irony is when the audience knows that Juliet isn't dead, but Romeo believes that she is.
      - Think of superheroes with a secret identity. The audience knows that Clark Kent is Superman, but somehow, because of some glasses, no one else does.
      - In the first Toy Story movie, the audience knows that Buzz Lightyear is a toy, but he's sure he's a space ranger.
      - (Notice the above examples are a Shakespearean play, the Justice League, and a Pixar movie. Clearly dramatic irony is useful across all genres.)

- Here are 5 ways irony can enhance your writing.
  - You can make your writing tenser by allowing your character to make mistakes that wouldn't be made if they could see the full picture (like Romeo and Juliet).

- You can make your character speak their mind to someone they don't recognize and reveal feelings they wouldn't otherwise have expressed (like Superman).
- You can make a character vulnerable by putting them in a circumstance they don't understand (like Buzz).
- You can use irony to add humor.
- Irony can help keep your reader engaged. They want to keep reading until the characters' knowledge catches up with their own as the reader.

- Things to avoid with irony in your writing:
  - Avoid making your irony so obvious that it makes your character look oblivious. This kind of character can become uninteresting to follow.
  - Avoid making your character do illogical things that turn into unintended humor. Humor is great, but you don't want people laughing when they're supposed to be scared or sad.

Now let's review foreshadowing.

- Foreshadowing is a way of hinting at what will come later.
  - It can be evidenced in all kinds of ways from the changes in the weather or scenery to the ways characters interact with one another.
  - It can be found in dialogue, in descriptions, etc.
  - Foreshadowing adds dramatic tension, builds suspense, and makes a literary work more interesting.

- Ways to add foreshadowing to your writing
  - Directly mention something that's upcoming.
    - God tells Noah to build an ark because it's going to rain.
  - Put clues at the beginning of the story or of a chapter that hint at themes that will be important later.
    - Romeo is established as impulsive from the beginning of Romeo and Juliet. The pair talk about preferring to die than to live without one another. Both of these things foreshadow what happens at the end of the play.
  - Using changes in the weather or mood can help subtly develop foreshadowing.
    - "The air was still, but he could tell it was the calm before the storm."
    - "Something about the way she spoke alerted others that there was a problem lying under the surface."

- Ways to find foreshadowing in a literary work
  - See if you can find phrases about the future.
  - See if you notice changes in weather, setting, or mood.
  - See if there are objects or scenic elements that suggest emotion of some kind: happy, sad, dangerous, exciting.
  - See if the characters observe subtle things that might be a hint about something to come.
  - Pay attention to the start of a story or chapter where foreshadowing often appears.

Fill in this irony chart as you're reading your short stories over the next few lessons. Fill in the definition of each type of irony and then write examples (and which story they came from).

Type of Irony	Definition of Type of Irony	Example of Irony
Verbal		
Situational		
Dramatic		

Lesson 32: Short Story Foreshadowing

Fill in this foreshadowing chart as you're reading your short stories over the next few lessons.

Event	Foreshadowing Used (clue that the event would happen)	Short Story

Continue to fill in your irony and foreshadowing charts as you read. What would you say is the theme of "The Story of an Hour"? How could you add dramatic irony to the story? Rewrite part of the story to add it in.

You are going to write a compare and contrast essay about two of the short stories you are reading. Here's a review about compare and contrast essays.

When comparing and contrasting ideas, you want to show how they are similar (compare) and different (contrast). There are many different methods you can use to help with this.

- Using a Venn Diagram or chart can help you quickly see the similarities and differences. A Venn Diagram utilizes overlapping circles that represent the items you are comparing and contrasting. In the overlapping section, you'll write ways they are similar. In the non-overlapping sections, you'll write the ways they differ from each other.

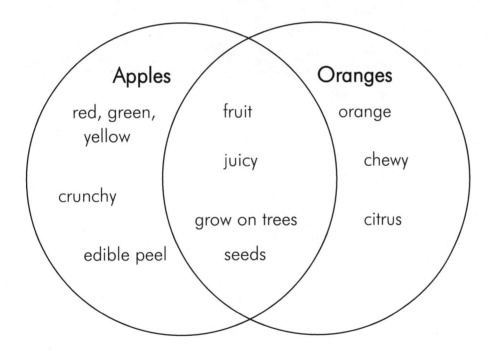

- A chart would list the characteristics of each part you want to compare. Those characteristics would go down the left side and the top would be the names of the items being compared. Once you fill in the boxes, it will be easy to find similarities and differences. Your chart can list many categories; this is just a simple example:

	Apples	Oranges
Color		
Cost		
Texture		
Other		

- Asking questions can also help you come up with comparisons and contrasts.
  - Ask: Who? What? Where? When? Why? How?
  - Consider general properties such as size, shape, color, location, duration.
  - Sensory details such as what something looks, feels, tastes, sounds, and smells like can also help, if applicable.
    - Comparing events
      - When did they occur?
      - How long did they last?
      - Why are they significant?
      - What people were involved?
      - What caused the events?
    - Comparing ideas
      - What are they about?
      - When did they originate?
      - Who created them or uses them?
      - How are they applied?
      - What kind of evidence is there for them?
    - Comparing writing or art
      - What are their titles?
      - What do they describe or depict?
      - What is their mood?
      - Who created them?
      - When were they created?
      - What type of setting/theme/tone or what type of art/period are employed?
    - Comparing two people
      - What are their demographics (age, race, gender, etc.)?
      - Where are they from?
      - What are their personalities/characteristics/beliefs?

- Once you have your brainstorming done, you need to narrow your focus.
  - What's relevant to the assignment? The course?
    - If you're comparing two pieces of writing for your literature class, their setting, characters, plot lines, etc. are going to be more important than the font they use. If you're comparing two pieces of writing for a typesetting class, the font becomes much more important.
  - What's interesting?
  - What supports the point you're trying to make?
  - What's the most important and needs to be mentioned no matter what?

- There are different ways to organize a compare and contrast essay.
  - Subject-by-subject
    - In this method, you say everything about one subject before moving on to say everything about the next subject (continuing if your essay contains more than two items or subjects being compared and contrasted).
      - This type of organization can be problematic because it turns your paper into a list of points instead of direct comparisons and contrasts between your subjects. Having a strong paragraph that ties all of your different points together is essential.
      - This type of structure is more beneficial when you're using one subject as a lens through which to view another. For instance, if you're given an assignment to compare *Romeo and Juliet*, which has been studied extensively in this course, to another poem of your choosing, you might point out specific things about *Romeo and Juliet* that then are similar or different to the poem of your choosing.
  - Point-by-point
    - This type of organization is probably the more popular way to write a compare and contrast essay. You address one point of comparison at a time and discuss how it plays out for each subject.
      - Depending on how much you have to say, you might discuss each point in separate paragraphs, or you might devote a paragraph for each point to each subject.
        - For instance, if I might compare the shape of apples and oranges in a single paragraph. If I had a lot more to say, I might discuss the shape of apples in one paragraph, then the shape of oranges in another.
  - Your own organization
    - There aren't really specific rules about organizing a compare and contrast paper, but as in any writing, you want your reader to be able to follow what you're saying.
    - The point you end with should be the most important point. If you determine the differences are more important than the similarities, end with the

differences. If you determine oranges are better than apples, don't end with a paragraph that shows where oranges are lacking in a certain point.

- Be clear in your points. Use words that demonstrate your purpose.
  - Like, unlike, similar, dissimilar, in the same way, on the contrary, conversely, similarly, on the one hand, on the other hand, etc. are all good cue words that show your reader where you're headed with what you're about to say.

Here's a sample compare and contrast essay from GAVL.

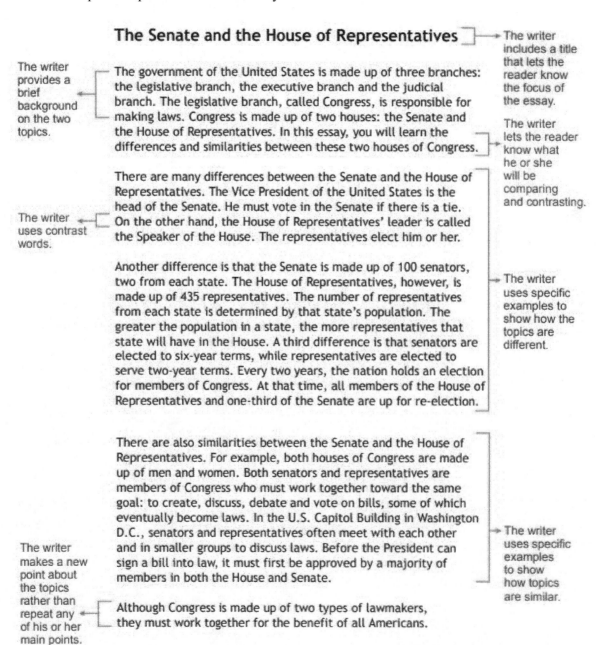

The Senate and the House of Representatives

The writer includes a title that lets the reader know the focus of the essay.

The writer provides a brief background on the two topics.

The government of the United States is made up of three branches: the legislative branch, the executive branch and the judicial branch. The legislative branch, called Congress, is responsible for making laws. Congress is made up of two houses: the Senate and the House of Representatives. In this essay, you will learn the differences and similarities between these two houses of Congress.

The writer lets the reader know what he or she will be comparing and contrasting.

The writer uses contrast words.

There are many differences between the Senate and the House of Representatives. The Vice President of the United States is the head of the Senate. He must vote in the Senate if there is a tie. On the other hand, the House of Representatives' leader is called the Speaker of the House. The representatives elect him or her.

Another difference is that the Senate is made up of 100 senators, two from each state. The House of Representatives, however, is made up of 435 representatives. The number of representatives from each state is determined by that state's population. The greater the population in a state, the more representatives that state will have in the House. A third difference is that senators are elected to six-year terms, while representatives are elected to serve two-year terms. Every two years, the nation holds an election for members of Congress. At that time, all members of the House of Representatives and one-third of the Senate are up for re-election.

The writer uses specific examples to show how the topics are different.

The writer makes a new point about the topics rather than repeat any of his or her main points.

There are also similarities between the Senate and the House of Representatives. For example, both houses of Congress are made up of men and women. Both senators and representatives are members of Congress who must work together toward the same goal: to create, discuss, debate and vote on bills, some of which eventually become laws. In the U.S. Capitol Building in Washington D.C., senators and representatives often meet with each other and in smaller groups to discuss laws. Before the President can sign a bill into law, it must first be approved by a majority of members in both the House and Senate.

The writer uses specific examples to show how topics are similar.

Although Congress is made up of two types of lawmakers, they must work together for the benefit of all Americans.

Write short examples of each type of irony. (You don't have to write out the story, just, "The main character thinks that... but...")

Record 3 points for each: 1 point for identifying the type of irony and 2 points for the example.

_____

_____

_____

_____

_____

_____

_____

_____

_____

_____

_____

_____

_____

Lesson 35: Compare and Contrast Essay Lit & Comp II LA

Finish your foreshadowing and irony charts. Give yourself 5 points for each completed chart.

Review these compare and contrast strategies for planning the structure of your essay.

Here are three strategies to organize compare and contrast essays (some we've already mentioned):

- **Whole-to-Whole, or Block**
  - o In this structure, you say everything about one item and then everything about the other.
    - ▪ For instance, say everything about the characters, setting, and plot for the one story then everything about the characters, setting, and plot for the other. The points in each of the sections should be the same and they should be explained in the same order.
      - • For instance, you might discuss character, setting, and plot for both, and in that order for both.

- **Similarities-to-Differences**
  - o In this structure, you explain all the similarities about the items being compared and then you explain all the differences.
    - ▪ For instance, you might explain that the characters and plot were similar in both stories or in a section of both stories. In the next section, you could explain that the settings were different.
      - • In other words, the body of your paper would have two large sections: one for similarities, another for differences.

- **Point-by-Point**
  - o In this structure, you explain one point of comparison before moving to the next point.
    - ▪ For instance, you would write about the characters in the two stories in one section, then you would write about the setting of the two stories in the next section. Point-by-Point comparison and contrast uses a separate section or paragraph for each point.
      - • Point #1 for your paper could be information about the characters in the two stories. You'd begin a section or paragraph for Point #2.
      - • For consistency, begin with the same item in each section of your point-by-point paper. For instance, for each point that you discuss, explain the information about Story A first and then about Story B.

- **Transition Words:** In compare and contrast essays, transition words tell a reader that the writer is changing from talking about one item to the other. Transitional words and phrases help make a paper smoother and more coherent by showing the reader the connections between the ideas that are being presented.

- o **To Compare:** When you're comparing items, using a transition word from this list will signal to readers that you're changing from one item to the next and it will also tell the reader that the two items are similar
  - Also
  - As
  - As well as
  - Both
  - In the same manner
  - In the same way
  - Like
  - Likewise
  - Most important
  - Same
  - Similar
  - Similarly
  - The same as
  - Too

- o **To Contrast:** On the other hand, using one of the transitions from this list of words will signal readers that the two items you're discussing are different.
  - Although
  - But
  - Differ
  - Even though
  - However
  - In contrast
  - Instead
  - Nevertheless
  - On the contrary
  - On the other hand
  - Unless
  - Unlike
  - While
  - Yet

Lesson 35: Compare and Contrast Rubric
Lit & Comp II LA

Keep this rubric in mind as you're writing your compare and contrast essay.

Total points possible = 25

1. **Purpose & Supporting Details (5 points)**
   - The paper compares and contrasts items clearly.
   - The paper points to specific examples to illustrate the comparison.
   - The paper includes only the information relevant to the comparison.

2. **Organization & Structure (5 points)**
   - The paper breaks the information into the whole-to-whole, similarities to-differences, or point by-point structure.
   - The paper follows a consistent order when discussing the comparison.
   - The paper breaks the information into appropriate sections or paragraphs to the ideas.

3. **Transitions & Coherence (5 points)**
   - The paper moves smoothly from one idea to the next.
   - The paper uses comparison and contrast transition words to show relationships between ideas.
   - The paper uses a variety of sentence structures and transitions.

4. **Conventions (5 points)**
   - The paper shows correct grammar and usage.
   - The paper follows the rules for punctuation.
   - The paper includes words that are spelled correctly.

5. **Sources (5 points)**
   - The paper contains quotes from stories to back up points (at least 3).
   - Quotations are correctly formatted according to MLA guidelines.
   - Works cited page is present and correctly formatted (should have entries for stories quoted).

(Adapted from GAVL, creative commons 3.0 [https://creativecommons.org/licenses/by/3.0/], http://cms.gavirtualschool.org/Shared/Language%20Arts/10thLitComp/03_ShortStoriesOne/ComparisonContrastRubric.pdf)

Use this Venn Diagram to compare and contrast the two stories you've chosen. Title each circle with the story it represents ("The Story of an Hour," "The Happy Prince," "Frederigo's Falcon").

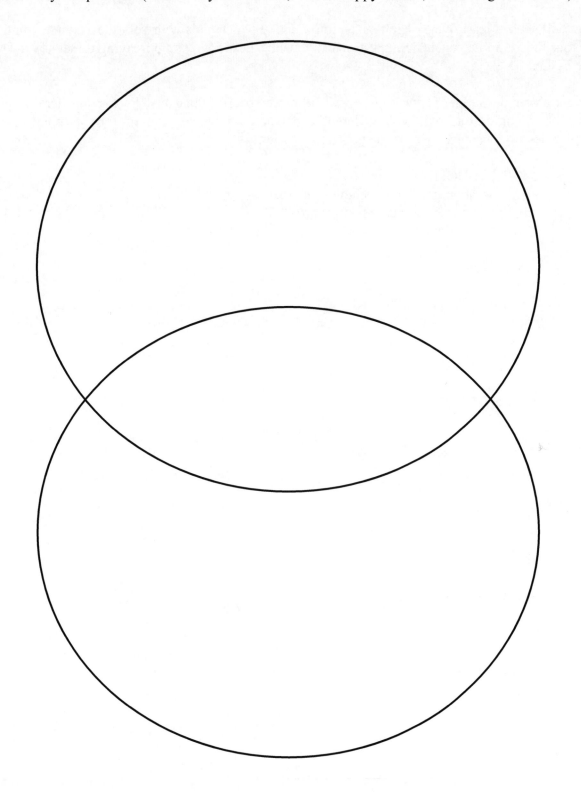

Create an outline for your compare and contrast essay. You should have a thesis statement as well as a topic sentence for each paragraph. You should also have quotes and examples for each point.

You will need at least five paragraphs: an introduction which ends with your thesis, three points that fit your thesis, and a conclusion that restates your thesis and wraps up, leaving us satisfied. This is due by Lesson 40.

Here's a sample outline. Your outline will be more specific than this. Each point here is just an example. Your outline will look different depending on which type of format (point-to-point, similarities-to-differences, etc.) you choose to go with.

    I.   INTRODUCTION
          a. Attention-grabbing opening sentence
          b. Stories to be compared and contrasted
               i. Story A
              ii. Story B
          c. Thesis

    II.   SUPPORTING POINT ONE
          a.
               i.
              ii.
          b.
               i.
              ii.

    III.   SUPPORTING POINT TWO
          a.
               i.
              ii.
          b.
               i.
              ii.

    IV.   SUPPORTING POINT THREE
          a.
          b.

    V.   CONCLUSION
          a. Restate thesis
          b. Wrap up

Lesson 37: Compare and Contrast Essay

Lit & Comp II LA

Work on your essay. It is due on Lesson 40. Use your outline from Lesson 36 and the rubric from Lesson 35.

Lesson 38: The Trojan War

Lit & Comp II LA

Work on your essay. It is due on Lesson 40. Use your outline from Lesson 36 and the rubric from Lesson 35.

Write a paragraph explaining the Trojan War, what you know of Odysseus, and what will happen after the war. Then complete the crossword puzzle.

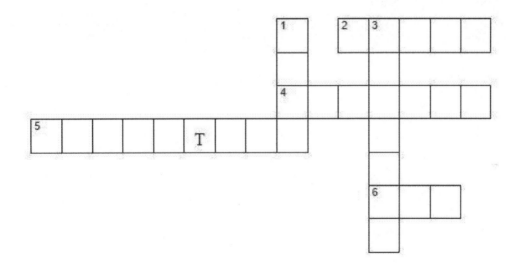

Across:
2. Took Helen back to Troy to marry her
4. An epic hero must possess traits that are important to _____.
5. A character that occurs in some stories across all cultures
6. The Trojan War lasted for _____ years.

Down:
1. A goddess who helps the main character in an epic poem
3. One of the characteristics of an epic poem is having a hero who has superhuman _____.

Read your essay out loud. Mark anything that sounds off or makes you stumble. There are online proofreaders if you want to run it through one (for example, paperrater.com/free_paper_grader). Edit your essay according to how it will be graded (see the rubric in Lesson 35). Your goal is to get a perfect score. On Lesson 40 you need to have your essay finished for grading.

Before you read each chapter (called "books") of *The Odyssey*, read the questions for the day. Fill in the answers here in the book *as your read*. You don't have to answer in complete sentences. Answer them like you're taking notes. You can just write O for Odysseus, for example.

Book I
1. Where is Odysseus in this book?

2. How is Athena disguised?

3. Why do Penelope and Telemachus need Odysseus?

4. Why does Penelope have suitors?

5. What advice does Athena give to Telemachus?

- Reread your essay and continue to edit it. Score your essay using the rubric in Lesson 35. Record your score out of 25.
- Give your essay to your peer editing partner, or at least to someone who can read it and give feedback. Send along the grading rubric (there's a link in the online course you can use if you want to).
  - Ideally, your peer editing partner is someone in your same grade. They don't have to use Easy Peasy. If you can't find someone like that among your family and friends, then ask someone older than you to read your essay and give you a grade.
- Give your editor the rubric and ask them for SPECIFIC feedback and a score out of 25. Record the score.
- Fix up your essay based on the feedback. Re-score your essay and multiply the grade by 4. Record your score out of 100.

Answer these questions as you read.

Book II
1. What trick does Penelope play on her suitors?

2. How does Athena help Telemachus?

Answer these questions as you read.

Book III

1. How does Nestor feel about Odysseus?

2. How does Nestor react when he realizes Athena is Telemachus' companion?

- You are going to write a short story. You get to be creative with the story, but you need to include irony, foreshadowing, and suspense!
- It doesn't have to be long. Think of how short "The Story of an Hour" was.
- Work on writing today. You will be editing and finishing on Lesson 45. Read over the grading rubric so you know what you're aiming for.
- Think about the diagram of a story from earlier:

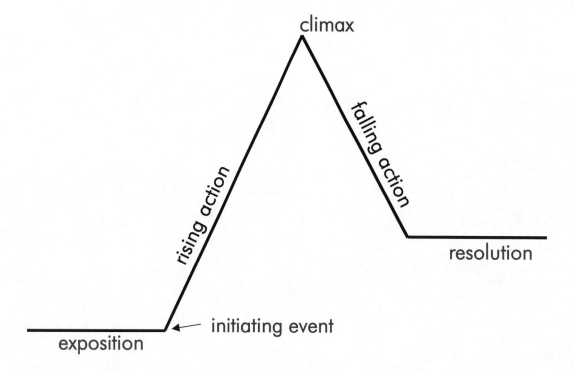

Lesson 41: Short Story Rubric

Here is the rubric you will use to grade your short story.

1. **Opening paragraph (4 points)**
   - 4 points – Captures reader's attention from the first paragraph without giving away too much
   - 3 points – Gets reader's attention in first paragraph, but hints too much about the story
   - 2 points – Lacks tension necessary to capture reader's attention and gives away too much of the story
   - 1 point – Has no creative tension to capture the reader and gives away the point of the story

2. **Writing (4 points)**
   - 4 points – Used creative and original ideas to create an interesting and unique story. Showed a clear desire and involved conflict in reaching that desire.
   - 3 points – Had some creative and original ideas with the start of an interesting story. Had a desire with some conflict reaching the desire.
   - 2 points – Had little creative ideas in the story. Unclear desire and little conflict to make an interesting story.
   - 1 point – Very little to no creative or original ideas. No real desire with very little to no conflict within the story.

3. **Word Choice (4 points)**
   - 4 points – Strong vocabulary using description in writing and word choice. Dialogue between characters is clear and easy to follow. Story is clear and easy to read.
   - 3 points – Some strong vocabulary showing description through word choice. Dialogue is a little difficult to understand. Story is easy to read with some confusing areas.
   - 2 points – Not a very strong use of vocabulary. Tells description rather than showing it. Dialogue is confusing to the reader. Story is a little difficult to understand.
   - 1 point – Dialogue is very confusing. Little to no strength in vocabulary. Little to no description in writing. Story is very confusing.

4. **Spelling, Grammar, Punctuation (4 points)**
   - 4 points – Little or no spelling, grammar, or punctuation errors.
   - 3 points – 5-7 spelling, grammar, and punctuation errors.
   - 2 points – 8-10 spelling, grammar, and punctuation errors.
   - 1 point – 11+ spelling, grammar, and punctuation errors.

5. **Suspense, Irony, Foreshadowing (4 points)**
   - 4 points – Utilizes all three literary devices
   - 3 points – Utilizes two of these literary devices
   - 2 points – Utilizes one of these literary devices
   - 1 point – Does not utilize these literary devices

Continue to work on your story. What clever moment can you put in? It is due on Lesson 45.

Answer these questions while you read.

Book IV
1. How do Helen and Menelaus realize Telemachus is Odysseus' son?

2. How does Menelaus feel about Odysseus?

3. How does Antinous plan to destroy Telemachus?

Lesson 43: The Odyssey Study Guide

Work on your story. Craft it. Does it have foreshadowing and irony? It is due on Lesson 45.

Answer these questions while you read.

Book V
1. Who does Zeus send to Calypso?

2. What is Hermes sent to do?

3. What can Hermes do with his wand?

4. How does Calypso feel about Hermes' message?

5. What happens when Odysseus leaves?

6. What happens at the end of this book?

Lesson 44: The Odyssey Study Guide

Work on editing your story. It is due on Lesson 45.

Answer these questions as you read.

Book VI
1. What does Athena influence Nausicaa to do while she sleeps?

2. What wakes Odysseus?

3. Why doesn't Nausicaa run away from Odysseus like the other girls?

4. What does Athena do for Odysseus after he bathes?

5. Why does Nausicaa make Odysseus follow behind the wagon?

6. What does Nausicaa tell Odysseus to do if he wants her father's help?

Work on creating a final draft of your short story. Score it using the grading rubric in Lesson 41. Multiply your score by 4 and record it out of 80.

Answer these questions as you read.

Book VII

1. What are the Phaeacians best known for?

2. How do they treat Odysseus?

STOP

This is the end of the first quarter. It's time to save some work in your portfolio. You should probably save all of your major written work: the literary analysis, the short story and the compare and contrast essay, and the poem too, if you like. At this point you can total up your scores from the first quarter (unless you are waiting on peer editing). Divide the total by the total possible and then multiply by 100 for your grade. (Just ignore decimals.) This is your first quarter grade. At the end of the year, we can add in points for completing the reading and daily assignments, but you should try for an A. Look at where you lost points and think about what you need to do to not lose them again.

Lesson 46: The Odyssey Study Guide

Answer these questions as you read. *(Remember to also be completing the lessons in your Reader and Vocabulary Workbook.)*

Book VIII

1. What activities does King Alcinous use to entertain Odysseus?

2. Who is Demodocus?

3. How does King Alcinous help Odysseus?

4. How does Odysseus react when Demodocus sings about the Trojan War?

Lesson 46: Verb Tense Agreement

Here's a review about verb tenses. (Note: in the example sentences below, verbs are <u>underlined</u> and inconsistent verbs are in **bold**.)

- Outside of very special circumstances, writers should choose one tense that is the main tense of their writing, and then only change tense if there is a change of time frame.

- If there is no change of time frame, the verb tense should be the same across the writing.
  - The coach <u>spells out</u> the game plan to the players who then **clarified** their individual roles.
    - Since the sentence starts in the present tense and there is no change of time frame, it should end in the present tense as well.
      - Corrected: The coach <u>spells out</u> the game plan to the players who then <u>clarify</u> their individual roles.
  - Tomorrow we **went** to the store, and later we <u>will go</u> to the concert.
    - The established time frame is future tense (tomorrow), so the past tense verb is incorrect.
      - Corrected: Tomorrow we <u>will go</u> to the store, and later we <u>will go</u> to the concert.

- If there is a change of time frame, the verb tense should change.
  - We still <u>enjoy</u> our patio set that we <u>bought</u> four years ago.
    - *Enjoy* is present tense (we still enjoy it now), but *bought* is past tense (we bought it four years ago, we are not still buying it even though we're still enjoying it).
  - Yesterday we <u>went</u> to the store and later we <u>will go</u> to the concert.
    - Now the established time frame is past tense (yesterday), but the concert is happening in the future.

- In formal writing or essays, some general guidelines exist. These aren't hard and fast rules, but just general guidelines.
  - Utilize past tense to narrate events or tell a story.
    - Narration can be done in the present tense to add dramatic flair, but if you narrate in the present tense, you'll want to consistently remain in the present tense, only making shifts when time frames change.
      - The present tense tends to be more difficult to write in consistently.
  - Use present tense to state facts and to discuss your own feelings on the author's ideas.
    - "I think…" "I agree…" "I disagree…"

- You can utilize perfect and progressive tenses to help differentiate time further.
  - Here's an example from Purdue's online writing lab:
    - By the time Tom noticed the doorbell, it had already rung three times. As usual, he had been listening to loud music on his stereo. He turned the stereo down

and stood up to answer the door. An old man was standing on the steps. The man began to speak slowly, asking for directions.[2]

- The progressive verbs *had been listening* and *was standing* show that those actions were underway while other actions took place.
    - The listening of the stereo was already happening when the doorbell rang.
    - The standing on the steps was already happening when the door was opened.
        - Further, the past perfect progressive *had been listening* shows action that began before the new action and continued as the new action began.

- To refer to earlier time frames, use the following guidelines.
    - If you're using the **past tense** as your primary tense, utilize the **past perfect tense** for earlier time frames ("had" and the past participle).
    - If you're using the **present tense** as your primary tense, utilize the **present perfect tense** for earlier time frames ("has" or "have" and the past participle).
    - If you're using the **future tense** as your primary tense, utilize the **future perfect tense** for earlier time frames ("will have" and the past participle).

- Note: aside from tense being consistent, remember to always make sure your verb matches your subject when it comes to being singular or plural.
    - Those girls don't <u>want</u> to stop twirling their ribbons.
        - The verb goes along with *girls* and should be a plural verb.
    - Neither of those girls twirling their ribbons <u>wants</u> to stop.
        - The verb goes along with *neither*, the singular indefinite pronoun.
        - *Of those girls* is a prepositional phrase that is not part of the subject.
    - Not only her shoes but also my shirt has mud on every square inch.
        - When you have "not only… but also" or "either… or" or a similar construction, the subject closer to the verb determines whether the verb is singular or plural. In this case, *shirt* is singular so the verb *has* is correct.

Do the verb tense exercises on the next page and then complete the graded quiz.

---

[2] "Verb Tense Consistency." *Purdue Online Writing Lab*, Purdue University, https://owl.purdue. edu/owl/general_writing/grammar/verb_tenses/verb_tense_consistency.html.

Lesson 46: Verb Tense Agreement

If the tense in the underlined verbs matches, place a check mark in the blank. If the tense needs to be corrected, put an X in the blank and fix the problem.

_____ If the game <u>starts</u> on time, it <u>would have finished</u> before my meeting.

_____ I <u>am</u> bummed it's raining today because I <u>had planned</u> to play outside.

_____ Everyone <u>thought</u> the flower <u>would live</u> longer.

_____ While we <u>visited</u> the zoo the giraffes <u>will be eating</u>.

_____ Chase <u>wants</u> to show us the play he <u>wrote</u>.

Fill in the blanks with a verb that fits the tense.

If the weather is warm enough, I want _____.

By the time my birthday rolls around, _____.

We left for the tournament as soon as _____.

When the final exams are graded, _____.

We gather together, wanting to _____.

Lesson 46: Verb/Subject Agreement Quiz

Choose the correct **present tense** verb for each sentence. When you're finished, check your answers and record your score out of 25.

1. Neither of those books _____ interesting to me.

    a. looks   b. look   c. looked   d. had looked

2. Cats and dogs chasing after him _____ William, but horses don't bother him.

    a. scares   b. scare   c. scared   d. had scared

3. Someone, maybe Holly or Liz, _____ the steps to solve the geometry problem.

    a. knew   b. knows   c. will know   d. know

4. The barking dogs and roaring train, coupled with the wind chimes playing in the wind each time it blows, _____ a noisy backdrop for the toddler's nap.

    a. made   b. has made   c. makes   d. make

5. The off brand soda _____ more than the on-sale name brand.

    a. costs   b. cost   c. will cost   d. had cost

6. Every pen and marker _____ run out of ink.

    a. will have   b. has   c. have   d. had

7. Not only my brother but also my friend's sisters _____ learned the song.

    a. will have   b. has   c. have   d. had

8. Either *Alias* or *Friends* _____ Jack's favorite TV show.

    a. was   b. were   c. are   d. is

(continued on next page)

9. Economics _____ become my favorite subject because it's easy for me.

    a. will have   b. has   c. have   d. had

10. There _____ the stack of papers I need you to file.

    a. is   b. are   c. was   d. were

11. Three cups of chopped cucumbers _____ like too much to me.

    a. seemed   b. had seemed   c. seems   d. seem

12. Where _____ the papers I left on the table?

    a. was   b. were   c. is   d. are

13. World Civilizations _____ been my hardest course this year.

    a. will have   b. has   c. have   d. had

14. The seven seats in our van _____ transportation for our eight-person family.

    a. complicated   b. will complicate   c. complicate   d. complicates

15. Everyone in the group, even Natalie and Caleb, _____ to go home early.

    a. wanted   b. have wanted   c. want   d. wants

16. At the local day care, all of the toddlers _____ right after lunch.

    a. napped   b. will nap   c. nap   d. naps

17. Two hundred and thirty dollars _____ too much to pay for the course.

    a. is   b. are   c. was   d. were

(continued on next page)

18. Mr. Ahlemeyer is one of those piano teachers who _____ on daily practice.

    a. insists   b. insist   c. insisted   d. has insisted

19. Where _____ the apples you wanted me to share?

    a. is   b. were   c. are   d. was

20. My mom and my dad _____ singing.

    a. enjoys   b. enjoy   c. enjoyed   d. will enjoy

21. Jessica's new pair of shoes _____ rubbed a blister on her feet.

    a. have   b. had   c. will have   d. has

22. The heavy traffic _____ maddening because I'm in a hurry.

    a. is   b. are   c. was   d. were

23. Each of the soccer players _____ the ball before lining up to start the game.

    a. touches   b. touch   c. touched   d. will touch

24. These pants _____ so wet that they won't have time to dry before we leave.

    a. is   b. are   c. has been   d. had been

25. Each first, second, third, and fourth grader _____ a part in the play.

    a. will have   b. had   c. have   d. has

Answer these questions as you read.

Book IX

1. What happened to someone who ate of the lotus?

2. How heavy was the door of the Cyclops' cave?

3. What does the Cyclops do instead of answering Odysseus?

4. Why doesn't Odysseus kill the Cyclops?

5. What gift does Odysseus give the Cyclops?

6. What "present" does the Cyclops offer in return?

7. How do the men sneak out of the cave?

(continued on next page)

8. What does Odysseus do after he escapes and returns to his ship?

9. How does the Cyclops respond?

10. What did a prophet once prophesy about the Cyclops?

11. What does the Cyclops ask of his father Poseidon?

Answer these questions as you read.

Book X
1. Who is the god of wind?

2. What favor does he do for Odysseus?

3. What do some of the men do that undoes what Aeolus had done for them?

4. What did the Laestrygonians do?

5. What did Circe do to some of the men?

6. Where does Circe send Odysseus?

Answer these questions as you read.

Book XI

1. How does Odysseus call the souls of the dead to himself?

2. Who is Teiresias?

3. What does Odysseus want from Teiresias?

4. What does Teiresias tell Odysseus about his fate?

5. What should Odysseus do to the suitors?

6. With whom does Teiresias say Odysseus should make peace?

7. How did Odysseus's mother die?

Lesson 49: Journal Prompts

You are going to be doing a ten-minute writing time each day. If you don't have a stopwatch or timer, there is one linked in the online course. Choose a topic from the list below (you'll use this list each time). Just write until the time is up. Today you can choose to do this by hand or by typing. Record your score out of five according to the rubric below.

A	5 points	3/4 of a page or 250 words
B	4 points	2/3 of a page or 200 words
C	3 points	1/2 of a page or 150 words
D	2 points	1/3 of a page or 100 words

Here are the prompts you can choose from:

Describe your perfect vacation.
How would you become friends with someone who didn't speak your language?
If you could do whatever you wanted to do right now, what would you do?
If you could have lived in another time period, which one would you choose and why?
If you could have one talent that you don't currently have, what would you want it to be?
If you could travel anywhere, where would you go, and why?
In 20 years, I will be…
Tell about an event in your life that changed you.
What are the most important things in your life?
What are the qualities that make a good friend?
What do you like most about yourself?
What do you like to do in your free time?
What do you think about when you can't sleep?
What do you think our world needs most?
What does "the grass is always greener on the other side of the fence" mean?
What is something you do well?
What is something you wish you could change about yourself?
What is your biggest fear?
What is your favorite book and why?
What is your favorite room in your home and why?
What is your favorite song and why?
What makes you laugh?
What was the best lesson your parent (grandparent, guardian, friend) ever taught you?
What would happen if children ruled the world?
What would happen if it really did rain cats and dogs?
What would happen if there were no rules?
What would you do if a friend asked you to keep a secret that was dangerous to keep?
What would you do if someone said you did something wrong and you didn't actually do it?
What would you do if you were the leader of your country?

Answer these questions as you read. Then set your timer and write for ten minutes. Choose another prompt from Lesson 49's list and score it according to the rubric.

Book XII

1. What happens to those who hear the song of the Sirens?

2. What does Circe instruct Odysseus to do to avoid hearing the Sirens?

3. How does Circe describe Scylla?

4. Why does Odysseus need to avoid Charybdis?

5. What did Odysseus not tell his men, for fear they would quit rowing?

6. What happened to Odysseus's men at the end of Book XII?

Lesson 51: The Odyssey Study Guide

Answer these questions as you read. Then set your timer and write for ten minutes. Choose another prompt from Lesson 49's list and score it according to the rubric.

Book XIII
1. How was Odysseus's journey home from Scheria?

2. What does Poseidon want to do to the Phaeacian ship?

3. What does Alcinous decide because of Poseidon's wrath?

4. Why does Athena want to disguise Odysseus?

5. What does Athena tell Odysseus to do now that he has returned to Ithaca?

Lesson 52: The Odyssey Study Guide

Answer these questions as you read. Then set your timer and write for ten minutes. Choose another prompt from Lesson 49's list and score it according to the rubric.

Book XIV

1. What is the swineherd's name?

2. What does the disguised Odysseus tell the swineherd about himself?

3. How is Odysseus disguised?

Lesson 53: The Odyssey Study Guide

Answer these questions as you read. Then set your timer and write for ten minutes. Choose another prompt from Lesson 49's list and score it according to the rubric.

Book XV

1. How has Eumaeus proven his faithfulness in this and previous books?

2. Who do you think will be the first person to know Odysseus for whom he really is?

Answer these questions as you read. Then set your timer and write for ten minutes. **Today, you must write by hand.** You need to practice for in-class written essays. They are on the SATs and will be part of many college courses. Choose another prompt from Lesson 49's list and score it according to the rubric.

Book XVI

1. What does Telemachus call Eumaeus?

2. What does Athena do for Odysseus's appearance?

3. What does Telemachus think when Odysseus comes back in and his disguise is removed?

4. What do Odysseus and Telemachus plan to do?

Lesson 55: The Odyssey Study Guide

Answer these questions as you read. Then set your timer and write for ten minutes. **Today, you must write by hand.** You need to practice for in-class written essays. They are on the SATs and will be part of many college courses. Choose another prompt from Lesson 49's list and score it according to the rubric. This will be for extra credit.

Book XVII

1. What does Telemachus tell Penelope to do when she sees that he has returned?

2. What does Theoclymenus prophesy to Penelope?

3. Who recognizes Odysseus immediately?

4. Who angers Odysseus?

5. Why doesn't Odysseus tell his servants and wife who he is right away?

Lesson 56: The Odyssey Study Guide Lit & Comp II LA

Answer these questions as you read. Then do the letter-writing assignment.

Book XVIII
1. Why does Odysseus fight Irus?

2. What does Penelope trick the suitors into giving her?

3. Other than Irus at the beginning, what other two characters anger Odysseus in this book?

- Write a letter from Odysseus to Penelope. Include parts of the story as you tell her what has happened to you.
- Give yourself 5 points for including each of the 5 parts of a friendly letter (heading, greeting, body, closing, signature) and 5 points for including details from the story in your letter.

Answer these questions as you read.

Book XIX

1. Disguised as the beggar, what does Odysseus tell Penelope about her husband?

2. How does Euryclea recognize Odysseus?

3. What happened to Odysseus that left him with a scar on his leg?

4. What is the tournament of axes?

Answer these questions as you read.

Book XX

1. Which two characters in this book treat Odysseus poorly because he is a beggar?

2. Who, in contrast, is kind to Odysseus the beggar?

3. What do you think Odysseus is going to do to the suitors?

Answer these questions as you read.

Book XXI

1. To whom does Odysseus reveal himself to get help in defeating the suitors?

2. Why do the suitors become very angry when Odysseus asks for a turn to try to string the bow?

3. How is the beggar finally revealed to be Odysseus?

Answer these questions as you read.

Book XXII

1. Whom does Odysseus kill first? Why do you think he chose him?

2. What does Eurymachus claim once he realizes who Odysseus really is?

3. Who is caught taking weapons from the storeroom? What happens to him?

4. Which servant begs to be spared? What second servant does Telemachus say should also be spared?

5. How does Odysseus figure out which of the maids have misconducted themselves?

6. What does Odysseus do to the unfaithful maids?

7. What happens to Melanthius?

Answer these questions as you read.

Book XXIII
1. How does Penelope test Odysseus to make sure it's him?

2. Why does Penelope test Odysseus?

3. What is the last task that Teiresias told Odysseus to complete? What will be his reward?

4. What does Odysseus leave to do? What does he tell Penelope to do?

Answer these questions as you read.

Book XXIV

1. How does Odysseus prove his identity to Laertes?

2. What is Laertes afraid will happen?

3. Who comes to get revenge on Odysseus?

4. Whom does Laertes kill?

5. Who stops the battle?

Lesson 63: The Odyssey Matching

Complete these matching activities and review your study guide as you prepare for a test covering the Odyssey in Lesson 64.

| Laestrygonians | Circe | Pig | Aeolus | Cyclops | Lotus-Eaters |

1. Gives Odysseus a bag containing all the winds. _____

2. Witch-goddess who lives in Aeaea. _____

3. The one-eyed monster through whose land they sail. _____

4. A group of giants. _____

5. In their land, some of Odysseus's men ate the plants and forgot about going home. _____

6. Circe turns Odysseus's men into these. _____

| beeswax | Calypso | Charybdis | Hermes | Scylla | Sirens |

1. Tells Odysseus to resist Circe by eating herb candy. _____

2. Six-headed monster who swallows sailors. _____

3. Odysseus returns to Circe, buries his man, then sails past these. _____

4. Odysseus uses this to plug ears against the Sirens. _____

5. Zeus punishes Odysseus and he ends up with no crew on her island. _____

6. A giant whirlpool that the ship encounters. _____

(continued on next page)

old beggar   Tiresias   home   Penelope   bed   Telemachus

1. Penelope finally believes Odysseus is her husband when he describes their _____.

   _____

2. As we leave the Odyssey, Penelope remains here while Odysseus leaves to make his final journey.

   _____

3. When Odysseus returns to Ithaca, he is disguised as this.

   _____

4. When he returns, _____ is fighting off suitors that have come to take control of his kingdom.

   _____

5. Eumaeus and this person are the only two who know that the beggar is Odysseus.

   _____

6. Odysseus must leave to make one final journey to fulfill what the prophet _____ told him to do.

   _____

Lesson 64: The Odyssey Test

Take this test on *The Odyssey*. There are 33 multiple choice questions worth 1 point each and 3 essay questions worth 4 points each. Give yourself 5 points if you read the WHOLE thing and didn't skip any "books." This will give you a total of 50 possible points.

1. The *main* story of the Odyssey is:

    a. Odysseus's influence with the gods   c. Odysseus's heroic deeds
    b. Odysseus's love of travel   d. Odysseus's loyalty

2. Which of these moments best demonstrates Odysseus's real, human side?

    a. He resists Circe's temptations.   c. He refuses to taste the Lotus plant.
    b. He weeps over his mother's ghost.   d. He plugs his men's ears with beeswax.

3. Which of these is an example of *simile*?

    a. Odysseus strung the bow in one motion.
    b. Odysseus watched the suitors like a captain surveying the angry sea.
    c. The suitors failed to string the bow.
    d. The Greek isles littering the ocean set the stage for the epic tale.

4. How do the Phaeacians help Odysseus?

    a. They give him a bag of winds.   c. They prophesy about his trip home.
    b. They provide him with food.   d. They give him a ship and treasures.

5. Through how many axes must the suitors shoot an arrow in Penelope's contest?

    a. thirty   .   c. eight
    b. twelve   d. seventeen

(continued on next page)

6. Which plant makes the sailors forget about wanting to return home?

    a. Lotus   c. Lily

    b. Hemlock   d. Poppy

7. Who or what is Argus?

    a. The leader of the suitors   c. The Cyclops

    b. Odysseus's old dog   d. A whirlpool

8. How does Euryclea recognize Odysseus?

    a. His voice   c. His eyes

    b. His craftiness   d. His scar

9. How does Odysseus safely listen to the Sirens' song?

    a. His men bind him to the ship's mast.   c. He is protected by Athena.

    b. He plugs his ears with beeswax.   d. He eats a Lotus plant.

10. How does Odysseus's mother die?

    a. old age   c. grief

    b. drowning   d. she's murdered

11. What does Tiresias warn Odysseus not to harm?

    a. the cattle of the Sun   c. the whirlpool

    b. the serpent   d. the Lotus plant

12. Who turns the sailors into pigs?

    a. Calypso   c. Scylla

    b. Poseidon   d. Circe

(continued on next page)

13. What does Odysseus do that angers Poseidon?

   a. disrespects the sea   c. attacks him
   b. blinds his son   d. tricks him with a disguise

14. Who rescues Odysseus from Calypso?

   a. Athena   c. Circe
   b. Nausicaa   d. Hermes

15. What does the death of Odysseus's dog emphasize?

   a. how long Odysseus has been gone   c. how loyal the dog is
   b. the dog doesn't love Odysseus   d. the dog is old

16. Where does Odysseus's journey take him (beginning and ending)?

   a. Sparta to Ithaca   c. Troy to Ithaca
   b. Sparta to Troy   d. Ithaca to Sparta

17. Which encounter does not result in the death of any of Odysseus's men?

   a. Laestrygonians   c. Scylla
   b. Lotus Eaters   d. Cyclops

18. Which of these places does Odysseus not visit?

   a. the realm of the gods   c. the island of cannibals
   b. the land of the dead   d. the cave of the Cyclops

19. Who was the last to find out that Odysseus was home?

   a. Penelope   c. Telemachus
   b. Laertes   d. Eumaeus

(continued on next page)

20. What is the name of the seer who returns to Ithaca with Telemachus?

    a. Theoclymenus   c. Eumaeus
    b. Tiresias   d. Laertes

21. Who offers Odysseus immortality?

    a. Athena   c. Circe
    b. Nausicaa   d. Calypso

22. Which god gave Odysseus a bag of winds?

    a. Poseidon   c. Aeolus
    b. Zeus   d. Hades

23. How many of Odysseus's men return to Ithaca with him?

    a. 0   c. 17
    b. 6   d. 10

24. Who awakens Odysseus while playing a game of ball?

    a. Arete   c. Euryclea
    b. Nausicaa   d. Athena

25. Who is the loyal swineherd?

    a. Melanthius   c. Eurystheus
    b. Demodocus   d. Eumaeus

26. Which of these best describes Penelope?

    a. stubborn   c. weak
    b. loyal   d. indecisive

(continued on next page)

27. Who prophesies a final task Odysseus must undertake?

   a. Theoclymenus   c. Eumaeus
   b. Tiresias   d. Laertes

28. From what war is Odysseus returning?

   a. Peloponnesian War   c. War with Sparta
   b. War on Mt. Olympia   d. Trojan War

29. For how many years is Odysseus held captive by Calypso?

   a. 20   c. 10
   b. 7   d. 1

30. How does Athena disguise Odysseus when he returns to Ithaca?

   a. a beggar   c. a child
   b. a suitor   d. a woman

31. For whom is Penelope weaving a shroud?

   a. Laertes   c. Odysseus
   b. Telemachus   d. Eumaeus

32. Who is Polyphemus?

   a. a Phaecean   c. a Lotus Eater
   b. Circe's servant   d. the Cyclops

33. What name does Odysseus give when he introduces himself to the Cyclops?

   a. Odysseus   c. Noman
   b. Zeus   d. Poseidon

(continued on next page)

Choose 3 questions to answer in a brief essay (paragraph). Support your answers with evidence from the story. Here's the rubric for these questions.

4 points	3 points	2 points	1 point
Effective elaboration; evidence from the story	Moderately well elaborated; some evidence from the story	Some elaboration; minimal evidence from the story	Unelaborated; no evidence from the story
Well-organized throughout	Organized with minor digressions	Gaps in organization	Unorganized
No errors in grammar, punctuation, or spelling	Few errors in grammar, punctuation, or spelling	Several errors in grammar, punctuation, or spelling	Many errors in grammar, punctuation, or spelling

1. How do Odysseus's men feel about him? Does it seem they regard him as a hero? Support your answer with evidence from the story.

2. Does Odysseus control his own destiny, or is his fate determined by the gods?

3. Tell how the story of *The Odyssey* might have ended differently if a character had chosen a different course of action in a certain part of the story.

4. If an epic hero shows the character traits that are most valued by the society in which they are written, describe the character traits most admired in ancient Greece based on the character of Odysseus.

5. You've been tasked with creating a screenplay of *The Odyssey*. Which two or three events would you focus on? Explain why they are the events that would most appeal to an audience, how they show Odysseus's character traits, and how they develop the themes of the epic.

Lesson 65: Journal Prompt Lit & Comp II LA

Set your timer and write for ten minutes. Choose another prompt from Lesson 49's list and score it according to the rubric.

Lesson 66: The Odyssey Essay Question Lit & Comp II LA

You have ten minutes to write an answer to one of the following essay questions. Start a timer when you are ready (this is practice for timed questions on the SAT or other tests). Your answer should be a complete paragraph. Your introduction should tell what you are going to be discussing in an interesting way. You should have several supporting sentences with examples from the book. Your conclusion should wrap up your point.

- Discuss the characters' attitudes toward strangers, including beggars and those visiting their home. How do they compare to Christian beliefs?
- What is the relationship of humans and gods in this story? How does it compare to Christian beliefs?
    - 2 points for the introduction if it states your main idea
    - 2 points for the conclusion if it restates your point
    - 2 points for each example from the book (use at least 2; chance for extra credit here)
    - 1 point for an interesting introduction
    - 1 point for a creative conclusion
    - Total: 10 points

Lesson 68: (no LA for Lesson 67) Journal Prompt Lit & Comp II LA

Set your timer and write for ten minutes. Choose another prompt from Lesson 49's list and score it according to the rubric.

Lesson 69: Newspaper Project

Write a newspaper article with a headline that would have appeared in a newspaper in Odysseus' day (if newspapers had existed back then). Choose an event from the book and write an article about it. Make sure you answer the who? what? where? when? and why? in your article. It is due on Lesson 71.

Your article should be <u>at least</u> three paragraphs, approximately 6-8 sentences each.

Grading Rubric (100 points possible)
1. Headline appropriate to content of book (10 points)
2. Who? (10 points)
3. What? (10 points)
4. When? (10 points)
5. Where? (10 points)
6. Why? (10 points)
7. Grammar/Spelling/Punctuation/etc. (10 points)
8. Content factually correct (20 points)
9. Article format & length (10 points)

Lesson 70: Newspaper Project

Work on your newspaper article. It is due on Lesson 71.

Lesson 71: Newspaper Project

Your newspaper article is due today. Use the rubric above to score your assignment. Record your grade on your grading sheet.

Read about pronouns.

Pronouns can come in many forms. Two of the main forms are subjective (or nominative) and objective. This chart shows the differences.

	Subjective	Objective
Singular	I, she, he, it	me, her, him, it
Plural	we, they	us, them
Singular and Plural	you, who	you, whom

- **Subjective pronouns**, as their name suggests, function as the subject of a sentence or clause.
    - Here are some examples.
        - <u>He</u> is a good teacher.
            - "He" is the subject of the sentence.
        - <u>She</u> wants to find someone <u>who</u> can teach her to play the guitar.
            - "She" is the subject of the independent clause
            - "who" is the subject of the dependent clause.

    - Subjective pronouns are also referred to as **nominative** because they can function as the predicate nominative.
        - <u>You</u> should remember that <u>it</u> was <u>he</u> <u>who</u> bought lunch.
            - "You" is the subject of the independent clause
            - "it" is the subject of the dependent clause
            - "he" is the nominative predicate to "it"
            - "who" is the subject of the final dependent clause.

- **Objective pronouns**, as their name suggests, function as the object of the sentence or clause.
    - Here are some examples.
        - Direct object:
            - My teacher likes <u>me</u>.
                - "teacher" is the subject of the sentence.
                - "me" is the direct object of the verb "likes"
            - Please take <u>her</u> to the bathroom.
                - "you" is the (implied) subject of the sentence
                - "her" is the direct object of the verb "take"
        - Indirect object:
            - Jessica offered Ashlyn and <u>me</u> a taste.
                - "Jessica" is the subject of the sentence
                - "taste" is the direct object of the verb "offered"
                - "Ashlyn" and "me" are the indirect objects

- When Isaac fell and skinned his knee, his mother gave <u>him</u> ice.
  - "mother" is the subject of the independent clause
  - "ice" is the direct object of the verb "gave"
  - "him" is the indirect object
- Object of a preposition:
  - Between <u>you</u> and <u>me</u>, this steak is tough.
    - "Between" is a preposition
    - "you" and "me" are objects of the preposition

- The subjective case should be used after "than" when the pronoun would use the same verb as the subject of the sentence in a comparison.
  - My friend likes orange juice more than <u>I</u>.
    - This sentence means my friend likes orange juice more than I like orange juice.
    - Incorrect: My friend likes orange juice more than <u>me</u> (objective).
      - This sentence means my friend likes orange juice more than my friend likes me.

- The objective case should be used after "than" if the pronoun doesn't compare or contrast with the subject, but is being compared or contrasted to an object or a complement.
  - She likes me better than <u>him</u>.
    - This means that she likes me better than she likes them.
    - She likes me better than <u>he</u> (subjective).
      - This means that she likes me better than he likes me.

- The subjective case should be used after "than" when the pronoun is being compared or contrasted to a quality of the subject.
  - <u>He</u> is happier than <u>she</u>.

- The objective case should be used after "than" if the comparison features a noun or pronoun with the adjective.
  - There is no happier person than <u>her</u>.
- The other most popular form of pronouns are **possessive pronouns**.
  - Some are paired with nouns: *my*, *your* (singular and plural), *his*, *her*, *its*, *their*, *our*.
    - That is <u>my</u> dog.
  - Others can stand alone: *mine*, *yours* (singular and plural), *his*, *hers*, *ours*, *theirs*.
    - That dog is <u>mine</u>.

Complete the pronouns exercises on the next page.

Lesson 72: Pronoun Activity

Choose the best form for the personal pronoun: subjective, objective, or possessive. These should be easy for you – just choose the word that fits – but be paying attention to the type of pronoun you're choosing to help you in future exercises. They're listed in order – each a choice is subjective, each b choices is objective, each c choice is possessive.

1. It's good that _____ can come with us.

      a. she   b. her   c. hers

2. You scratched _____ car.

      a. I   b. me   c. my

3. _____ scored more baskets than anyone else.

      a. He   b. Him   c. His

4. We should invite _____ to our game night.

      a. they   b. them   c. theirs

5. We decided that resting was in _____ best interest.

      a. we   b. us   c. our

6. Emily knew that it was up to _____ to get everyone to safety.

      a. she   b. her   c. hers

7. Would you like to come with _____ to the store?

      a. I   b. me   c. my

Choose the correct pronoun to fill in the blank. If you need help, try to determine if the needed pronoun should be a subject, object, or possessive pronoun.

It was _____ who folded all of that laundry.

    me   myself   I

My dad asked my brother and _____ to do our chores.

    me   myself   I

Meg and _____ spent the entire day playing cards.

    me   myself   I

My mom was not happy with _____ inviting several friends over without asking.

    me   myself   my

Between you and _____, that dinner could have been a lot better.

    me   myself   I

_____ spent all night on the phone together.

    She and Melanie   Melanie and her

_____ friendship is important to me.

    Jennifer's and my   Me and Jennifer's   Myself and Jennifer's

Are you upset with _____ choosing of the movie?

    me   myself   my

When it comes to haircuts, I like yours better than _____.

    mine   mines   mine's

Lesson 74: Pronouns

Try this exercise on pronoun agreement. Choose the correct answer to fill in each blank. Check your answers and learn from any mistakes you make. This is definitely harder! Remember what you learned in Lesson 46 about verb/subject agreement for words like neither, either, not only, etc. and see if that helps you with some of these.

1.   Either the teacher or your dad needs to give _____ permission.

              his   their

2.   With some effort, her stained shorts were restored to _____ clean condition.

              its   their

3.   Every one of the books was missing _____.

              its dust jacket   their dust jackets

4.   Both the book and the table got _____ cleaned after the spill.

              its surface   their surfaces

5.   Neither of my sisters put away _____ laundry today.

              her   their

6.   Each member of the men's group got to cast _____ vote.

              his   their

7.   Both the dog and the cat tried to assert _____ dominance.

              its   their

8.   The team of girls left _____ mark throughout the tournament.

              its   their

Lesson 75: Pronouns

Here's more practice on pronoun agreement. Choose the correct answer to fill in each blank. Check your answers and learn from any mistakes you make.

1. The family opted to cancel _____ family reunion when everyone got sick.

    its   their

2. Either my sister or my aunts will offer _____ home for our meal.

    her   their

3. Not only the mosquitoes but also that fly better not flap _____ wings in my ear anymore!

    its   their

4. Each daughter, mother, and grandmother in attendance was recognized for _____ accomplishments.

    her   their

5. That cat, as well as all of those dogs, better keep _____ paws off my lawn.

    its   their

6. I need the scissors and I can't find _____.

    it   them

7. Both Ethan and Caleb wanted _____ steak cooked medium well.

    his   their

8. The committee decided to postpone _____ meeting.

    its   their

Lesson 76: Journal Prompt

Set your timer and write for ten minutes. Choose another prompt from Lesson 49's list and score it according to the rubric.

Lesson 77: Journal Prompt

Set your timer and write for ten minutes. Choose another prompt from Lesson 49's list and score it according to the rubric.

Lesson 78: Journal Prompt

Set your timer and write for ten minutes. Choose another prompt from Lesson 49's list and score it according to the rubric.

Lesson 80: (no LA for lesson 79) Journal Prompt

Set your timer and write for ten minutes. Choose another prompt from Lesson 49's list and score it according to the rubric.

Lesson 81: Journal Prompt

Set your timer and write for ten minutes. Choose another prompt from Lesson 49's list and score it according to the rubric.

Lesson 82: Journal Prompt

Set your timer and write for ten minutes. Choose another prompt from Lesson 49's list and score it according to the rubric.

Lesson 83: Journal Prompt

Set your timer and write for ten minutes. Choose another prompt from Lesson 49's list and score it according to the rubric.

Lesson 84: Journal Prompt

Set your timer and write for ten minutes. Choose another prompt from Lesson 49's list and score it according to the rubric.

Lesson 85: Journal Prompt

Set your timer and write for ten minutes. Choose another prompt from Lesson 49's list and score it according to the rubric.

Lesson 86: Journal Prompt

Set your timer and write for ten minutes. Choose another prompt from Lesson 49's list and score it according to the rubric.

Lesson 87: Journal Prompt

Set your timer and write for ten minutes. Choose another prompt from Lesson 49's list and score it according to the rubric.

Lesson 88: Journal Prompt

Set your timer and write for ten minutes. **Today, you must write by hand**. You need to practice for in-class written essays. They are on the SATs and will be part of many college courses. Choose another prompt from Lesson 49's list and score it according to the rubric.

Lesson 89: Journal Prompt

Set your timer and write for ten minutes. **Today, you must write by hand**. You need to practice for in-class written essays. They are on the SATs and will be part of many college courses. Choose another prompt from Lesson 49's list and score it according to the rubric.

Lesson 90: Character Matching

Lit & Comp II LA

Do you know who these characters are? The list of possible answers is in the box. Use the internet to search if you don't know one.

Arthur	Guinevere	Merlin	Sir Gawain
Sir Kay	Sir Galahad	Sir Mordred	

Foster brother of King Arthur

_____

Illegitimate son of Arthur; traitor

_____

Sat in the siege perilous; went on quest for Holy Grail

_____

Knight of Arthur's court who was attractive and a ladies' man

_____

Wife of King Arthur

_____

Arthur's adviser and magician

_____

Great king of Britain

_____

STOP

This is the end of the second quarter. It's time to save some work in your portfolio. You should probably save all of your major written work: your newspaper article would be the big one from this quarter. You could also save a journal writing page or two. You can save a vocabulary quiz or activity to show what you are doing. At this point you can total up your scores from the second quarter. Divide the total by the total possible and then multiply by 100 for your grade. (Just ignore decimals.) This is your second quarter grade. At the end of the year, we can add in points for completing the reading and daily assignments, but you should try for an A. Look at where you lost points and think about what you need to do to not lose them again.

Lesson 90: Camelot/Kennedy Essay

Read the following excerpt from eNotes about the Kennedy presidency and the connection to Camelot.

The term "Camelot" was applied to the presidency of John F. Kennedy (1917-1963) by his wife, Jacqueline Bouvier Kennedy (1929-1994). Camelot refers to the seat of the court of the legendary King Arthur and the Knights of the Round Table; it has come to mean a place or time of idyllic happiness… Shortly after John F. Kennedy was assassinated on November 22, 1963, the former first lady was talking with a journalist. She described the years of her husband's presidency (1960-63) as an American Camelot, a period of hope and optimism in U. S. history, and asked that his memory be preserved. She had shown fortitude (ability to deal with adversity or pain) and grace as she guided her family and the country through the president's funeral and was one of America's most beloved first ladies. [3]

- Your task is to do a little more research about this Camelot connection. Then write an essay that compares the Kennedy presidency to Camelot, and/or the legends of King Arthur and his court. Be sure to include examples from the texts that you read in this unit. You may use other Arthurian texts as well. Remember to make sure they are cited correctly.

Essay Requirements:

1. At least 500 words
2. At least 3 examples from Arthurian literature to support your opinion
3. At least 2 quotes from other sources to support your opinion
4. MLA formatted in-text citations for sources used (for literature and outside sources)
5. MLA formatted works cited page
6. A strong introduction and conclusion
7. Use 3<u>rd</u> person (he, she, him, her, they, them). *Do not use the first person* in your paper ("I" or "my").

(Assignment, including enotes excerpt, from GAVL, creative commons 3.0 [https://creativecommons.org/licenses/by/3.0/], http://cms.gavirtual school.org/ Shared/Language%20Arts/10thLitComp/06_TheArthurianLegends/10Lit_ArthurianLegends_SOFTCHALK5.html)

- You'll need to do your own research for this project. There are links in the online course on lesson 90 that you can read or you can use other sources. If you need a refresher in MLA formatting, flip back to lesson 2.

- Today, read through some sources and start thinking about what you are going to write. Take down some notes. Read through the rubric on the next page to know what is expected of you. Aim for a perfect score in each category!

---

[3] https://www.enotes.com/homework-help/why-kennedy-presidency-called-camelot-287666

Lesson 90: Camelot/Kennedy Essay Rubric Lit & Comp II LA

Here's the rubric you'll use to grade your essay.

1. **Purpose and Focus (20 points)**
   1. 20 points – Establishes and maintains clear focus; evidence of distinctive voice and/or appropriate tone
   2. 19-13 – Focused on a purpose; evidence of voice and/or suitable tone
   3. 12-6 – An attempt to establish and maintain purpose and communicate with the audience
   4. 5-1 – Limited awareness of audience and/or purpose

2. **Development of Ideas (20 points)**
   1. 20 points – Depth and complexity of ideas supported by rich, engaging, and/or pertinent details; evidence of analysis, reflection and insight
   2. 19-13 – Depth of idea development supported by elaborated, relevant details
   3. 12-6 – Unelaborated idea development; unelaborated and/or repetitious details
   4. 5-1 – Minimal idea development, limited and/or unrelated details

3. **Sources (10 points)**
   1. 10 points – Use of references indicate substantial research
   2. 9-6 – Use of references indicate ample research
   3. 5-3 – Some references
   4. 2-1 – Few references

4. **Organization (20 points)**
   1. 20 points – Careful and/or suitable organization
   2. 19-13 – Logical organization
   3. 12-6 – Lapses in focus and/or coherence
   4. 5-1 – Random or weak organization

5. **Sentence Structure (10 points)**
   1. 10 points – Variety of sentence structure and length
   2. 9-6 – Controlled and varied sentence structure
   3. 5-3 – Simplistic and/or awkward sentence structure
   4. 2-1 – Incorrect or lack of topic and/or ineffective wording and/or sentence structure

6. **Grammar and Formatting (10 points)**
   1. 10 points – Control of surface features
   2. 9-6 – Few errors in grammar or format relative to length and complexity
   3. 5-3 – Some errors in grammar and/or format that do not interfere with communication
   4. 2-1 – Errors in grammar and format (e.g., spelling, punctuation, capitalization, headings)

7. **Language (10 points)**
   1. 10 points – Precise and/or rich language
   2. 9-6 – Acceptable, effective language
   3. 5-3 – Simplistic and/or imprecise language
   4. 2-1 – Incorrect and/or ineffective wording and/or sentence structure

Lesson 91: Camelot/Kennedy Essay

Make an outline for your paper. Include in your outline the examples and quotes you are going to use (and make sure you record where the quotes are from). Flip back to Lesson 90 if you need a refresher on the assignment. *(Remember to also be completing the lessons in your Reader and Vocabulary Workbook.)*

Lesson 92: Camelot/Kennedy Essay

Start writing. You will finish writing on Lesson 93.

Lesson 93: Camelot/Kennedy Essay

Finish writing. (You can still edit.)

Lesson 94: Camelot/Kennedy Essay

- Edit your paper. Use the rubric in Lesson 90 to make sure you got it right.
- Score your paper based on the rubric.
- Record your score. If you don't finish today, take 10 points off for each extra day it takes you to finish. You have to get your work in on time!
- Continue Lesson 94 on the next page.

Read about parallel form.

- Using parallel form or parallel structure means using the same pattern of words in order to show that multiple ideas have the same level of importance.
  - Julius Caesar said "I came, I saw, I conquered."
    - Which of these three things is the most important? Easiest?
      - They're all the same level of importance. They're all equally easy.
  - Abraham Lincoln uses prepositional phrases to express the American democracy in parallel form:
    - "…of the people, by the people, for the people."

- In parallel form, you want to keep the forms of your words, phrases, or clauses the same.

- Examples of words/phrases in parallel form:
  - Parallel: Caroline's hobbies include reading, writing, and singing.
  - Parallel: Caroline likes to read, to write, and to sing.
  - Parallel: Caroline likes to read, write, and sing.
    - Don't mix these up!
      - Not parallel: Caroline likes to read, to write, and singing.
      - Not parallel: Caroline likes reading, writing, and to sing.
  - Parallel: She did her job quickly, accurately, and efficiently.
    - Not parallel: She did her job quickly, accurately, and in an efficient manner.

- Examples of clauses in parallel form:
  - Parallel: We stress to our children that they should eat healthy meals, that they should get plenty of sleep, and that they should spend time exercising.
    - Not parallel: We stress to our children that they should eat healthy meals, to get plenty of sleep, and that they should spend time exercising.
  - Parallel: My favorite activities are either reading books or watching TV.
    - Not parallel: My favorite activities are either reading books or to watch TV.
- Certain words naturally pair together such as either/or, neither/nor, both/and, not only/but also. When you use these pairs (called **correlatives**), be sure the words/phrases/clauses following each part of the pair of is parallel.
  - Parallel: She was captivated by not only the sights but also the sounds.
    - Not parallel: She was captivated by not only the sights, but also it was the sounds.

- How would we correct the faulty parallelism in these sentences?
  - The friends decided to go to lunch and then that they would catch a movie.
    - The friends decided to go to lunch and then to catch a movie.
  - A great day for me is a big window nook and I would like a book to read.
    - A great day for me is a big window nook and a book to read.

Lesson 94: Parallel Form

Answer whether each sentence is parallel or not parallel. Record your score out of 9 (chance for an extra credit point).

1.   He wanted to go to the post office and eating lunch.

   parallel   not parallel

2.   Ethan grabbed his keys, found his sunglasses, and left the house.

   parallel   not parallel

3.   Stuart was amazed at not only the sunset, but also the starry sky.

   parallel   not parallel

4.   Evelyn wants the chocolate chip cookie but also is wanting cake.

   parallel   not parallel

5.   The dog was furry, happy, and hyper.

   parallel   not parallel

6.   She proposed that we go for a run and then we should stop for smoothies.

   parallel   not parallel

7.   When Amy gets home she likes either cooking dinner or to take a bath.

   parallel   not parallel

8.   My sister gave me not only a high five but also a hug when I fixed her lunch.

   parallel   not parallel

9.   Some people say that being smart is the same thing as to get good grades.

   parallel   not parallel

10.   Did you choose to come in because it is raining or were you done playing?

   parallel   not parallel

Lesson 95: Nonfiction

Your reading lesson for the day talks about nonfiction. Here are some examples and types of nonfiction. This is not an exhaustive list, but gives plenty of examples of the varied forms of nonfiction writings.

- Autobiography or biography
  - A writing about someone's whole life with the purpose to inform.

- Memoir
  - Focuses on one part of the author's life.

- Catalogue
  - A compilation of products available from a company with the purpose to persuade to purchase.

- Diary or journal
  - Writings recounting certain events in chronological order with the purpose of preserving them, informing, and entertaining.

- Encyclopedia
  - Information organized alphabetically by topic with the purpose to inform.

- Essay
  - Depending on the type, information is based on research or personal experience with the purpose to inform, persuade, or entertain.

- Feature story
  - A story about a single topic or main idea with the purpose to inform or entertain.

- Instructions
  - Writing that tells you step-by-step how to do, make, or fix something.

- Interview
  - A word-for-word account with the purpose to inform or entertain.

- Newspaper articles
  - Short writings that focus on one topic or main idea with the purpose to inform or persuade.

- Pamphlets
  - Usually one folded page with the purpose of informing or persuading.

- Textbook
  - Information organized by topic or chronologically with the purpose to inform.

Match each example to the type of nonfiction it represents.

_____ 1. Article   A. Frederick Douglass wrote about his life

_____ 2. Autobiography   B. "Angela's Ashes" by Frank McCourt (recounts his experiences during his impoverished childhood)

_____ 3. Biography   C. A principal addresses the student body of her school

_____ 4. Diary   D. A book about Edgar Allan Poe's life

_____ 5. Memoir   E. A New York Times Newspaper piece

_____ 6. Speech   F. Anne Frank's daily, chronological accounts of her experiences

- Your next assignment will be writing a biography.

  - You can start thinking about whom you'd like to write about.
  - Include 500-700 words, in paragraph form, with MLA formatting.
  - Use at least 3 sources to find information. (Remember to look for valid websites.)
  - Use in-text citations (at least 4).
  - Include a correctly formatted MLA works cited page.
  - Cover details about the person's birth/death, early influences, education, major accomplishments, and significance.
  - Write in the 3rd person.

Read about writing a biography.

- A biography is the story of a life.
  - They are usually about famous/infamous people, but can also be written about ordinary people.
  - They are more often about historical figures but can be about people still living.

- Biographies are written in chronological order or by themes.
  - Theme examples: achievements, historical impact, cultural shaping

- Biographers use both primary and secondary sources as they research.
  - Primary sources: letters, diaries, newspaper accounts
  - Secondary sources: other biographies, reference books or other histories.

- Steps to writing a biography:
  - Choose a person you are interested in learning more about.
  - Research basic facts about the person's life. Encyclopedias are a good place to start, as are credible internet sources (see Lesson 4).
  - After compiling basic facts and learning a bit about the person, think about what parts of their life you'd like to know more about/write about. Think about things like:
    - What makes this person interesting?
    - What events shaped them?
    - What impact did they have on the world?
    - How would you describe them?
    - What examples from their life give reasons you would describe them in that way?
    - Did they overcome some obstacle, take risks, etc.?
  - Continue your research to answer the above questions.
  - Write your biography, following the things you know about effective essay writing.

- Tips to make your biography more interesting to read:
  - Remember that a biography is a story, a narrative. Include details so your readers can imagine the events unfolding. People, places, and events should be included.
  - Create a purpose – why are you writing about this person in particular?
  - Don't jump around chronologically unless it makes sense to do so because there are definite themes that you're tracing through the person's life. In general though, you're telling a life story and life moves chronologically.
    - Your introduction and conclusion can be excluded from this tip due to the nature of those paragraphs.
  - Create a thesis or claim just like you would in any other essay. This will help your readers know where you're going with your essay and allow them to stay more engaged.

Here is a sample biography. Be sure to read all of the notes in the margins.

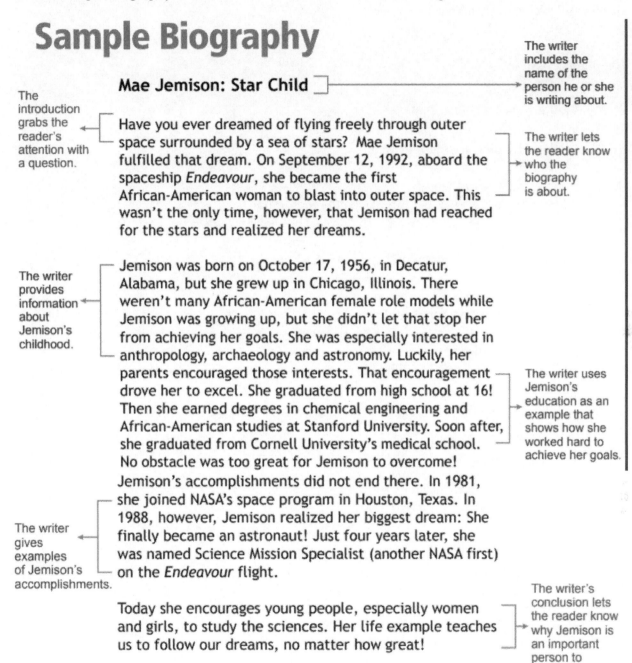

Sample Biography

Mae Jemison: Star Child

The writer includes the name of the person he or she is writing about.

The introduction grabs the reader's attention with a question.

Have you ever dreamed of flying freely through outer space surrounded by a sea of stars? Mae Jemison fulfilled that dream. On September 12, 1992, aboard the spaceship *Endeavour*, she became the first African-American woman to blast into outer space. This wasn't the only time, however, that Jemison had reached for the stars and realized her dreams.

The writer lets the reader know who the biography is about.

The writer provides information about Jemison's childhood.

Jemison was born on October 17, 1956, in Decatur, Alabama, but she grew up in Chicago, Illinois. There weren't many African-American female role models while Jemison was growing up, but she didn't let that stop her from achieving her goals. She was especially interested in anthropology, archaeology and astronomy. Luckily, her parents encouraged those interests. That encouragement drove her to excel. She graduated from high school at 16! Then she earned degrees in chemical engineering and African-American studies at Stanford University. Soon after, she graduated from Cornell University's medical school. No obstacle was too great for Jemison to overcome!

The writer uses Jemison's education as an example that shows how she worked hard to achieve her goals.

The writer gives examples of Jemison's accomplishments.

Jemison's accomplishments did not end there. In 1981, she joined NASA's space program in Houston, Texas. In 1988, however, Jemison realized her biggest dream: She finally became an astronaut! Just four years later, she was named Science Mission Specialist (another NASA first) on the *Endeavour* flight.

Today she encourages young people, especially women and girls, to study the sciences. Her life example teaches us to follow our dreams, no matter how great!

The writer's conclusion lets the reader know why Jemison is an important person to learn about.

Lesson 98: Biography Rubric

Lit & Comp II LA

Here is your rubric for your biography assignment. Refer to it as you're researching and writing and aim for full points in each area.

100 points possible

1. 5 points: Birth Date/Birthplace

2. 5 points: Death Date/Place of Death

3. 15 points: Early Influences
   (Must include 3 events that influenced the individual.)

4. 15 points: Education
   (Must include its role or significance in later life.)

5. 20 points: Major Accomplishments
   (Must provide dates if applicable.)

6. 20 points: Significance
   (Must explain why this individual is worthy of note in their field of expertise.)

7. 15 points: Grammar and Spelling
   (Each error results in one point off.)

8. 5 points: Neatness

As a reminder, your assignment is as follows:

- Include 500-700 words, in paragraph form, with MLA formatting.
- Use at least 3 sources to find information. (Remember to look for valid websites)
- Use in-text citations. (at least 4)
- Include a correctly formatted MLA works cited page.
- Cover details about the person's birth/death, early influences, education, major accomplishments, and significance.
- Write in the 3rd person.

Research your topic. Remember about choosing quality sources!

(Rubric adapted from GAVL, creative commons 3.0 [https://creativecommons.org/licenses/by/3.0/], http://cms.gavirtualschool.org/Shared/Language%20Arts/10thLitComp/05_NonfictionOne/Biography_Rubric.pdf)

Lesson 99: Story Elements

Fill in what you can of this story elements worksheet for "The Adventure of the Noble Bachelor."

Setting
Place: _____

Time: _____

Weather: _____

Social conditions: _____

Mood/atmosphere: _____

Plot
Introduction: _____

Rising action: _____

Climax: _____

Falling action: _____

Denouement/outcome: _____

Conflict
External: _____

Internal: _____

Physical (man vs. man): _____

(continued on next page)

Classical (man vs. circumstances): _____

Social (man vs. society): _____

Psychological (man vs. himself): _____

Character – describe the main characters in one or two sentences

Character 1: _____

_____

Character 2: _____

_____

Character 3: _____

_____

Point of View – In which point of view was the story written and how do you know?

_____

_____

_____

_____

Theme – Describe the theme of the story and then tell why you say that.

_____

_____

_____

_____

Choose whether each sentence is parallel or nonparallel.

1. Dustin ate broccoli, mashed potatoes, and skipped the turkey.

    parallel   not parallel

2. Elizabeth was making a grocery list, checked the fridge, and looked in the pantry before heading to the store.

    parallel   not parallel

3. Patricia types quickly, reads speedily, and forgets easily.

    parallel   not parallel

4. Bears that roar, growling leopards, and screeching eagles created a cacophony at the zoo.

    parallel   not parallel

5. Neither the pelting of the rain nor the blowing of the wind could keep Andrew from playing outside.

    parallel   not parallel

Choose the sentence from each group that is parallel.

6. ◯ Janet is a mathematician but who works at the grocery store at night.
    ◯ Stuart is loud, boisterous, and a hyper child.
    ◯ Stephanie not only walked the walk but also talked the talk.

7. ◯ I always have read and will read nonfiction twice a month.
    ◯ Running, hiking, and skiing are Jenn's favorite outdoor activities.
    ◯ Bird watching, relaxing, and a brisk walk are Holly's favorites.

8. ◯ I hope to visit either Rome or Paris.
    ◯ By noon I want either to eat lunch or to be sleeping.
    ◯ I desire either to run a marathon or swim a 100-meter freestyle race.

Lesson 99: Biography

1. Research. Look for quotes. Write down the sources!
2. Work on your outline.
3. Include your quotes and sources.
4. This assignment is due on Lesson 105.
5. You will not be told what to do each day. You will have other language arts assignments and be expected to remember to work on your biography as well without being reminded. You will research, outline, write, edit and finalize. Use your directions and your rubric. Manage your time and be smart about it. Don't leave it for the last day.

Lesson 100: Journal Prompt

Set your timer and write for ten minutes. **Today, you must write by hand**. You need to practice for in-class written essays. They are on the SATs and will be part of many college courses. Choose another prompt from Lesson 49's list and score it according to the rubric.

Lesson 101: MLA Formatting

Refresh your memory on how to set up MLA formatting by reviewing Lesson 2. If you'd like to view other sample papers you can check the online course.

Lesson 102: Citing Sources

Here's a general reminder about citing sources using MLA. A more comprehensive overview can be found in Lesson 2.

- When creating your Works Cited page, no matter the publication, there is a specific order and punctuation to the information. It should follow this order. Not all items will apply to each work you're citing. Just skip in order down to the next one you need.
    - Author.
    - Title of source.
    - Title of container,
    - Other contributors,
    - Version,
    - Number,
    - Publisher,
    - Publication date,
    - Location.

The online writing lab at Purdue can be a good online source for getting any specific MLA questions answered. That can be found at owl.perdue.edu.

Flip back to Lesson 5 and refresh your memory on literary analysis and writing a thesis.

Refresh your memory on plagiarism by taking the quiz again. Record up to 5 points on your grade sheet.

1. Plagiarism can be avoided by thoroughly citing sources.　　True　　False

2. Ideas cannot really be stolen.　　True　　False

3. You can use a Works Cited list for listing the sources you've used.　　True　　False

4. If you paraphrase or summarize a document, you don't have to cite the source.　　True　　False

5. Sometimes something popular, like playing covers of copyrighted songs, can still be considered plagiarism.　　True　　False

Lesson 102: Literary Terms Quiz

Take this quiz on literary terms. Record up to 10 points out of 5 (possible extra credit).

1. This refers to the struggle, usually between the protagonist and antagonist.

    a. setting   b. theme   c. conflict

2. A character who tells a story is a _____.

    a. character   b. narrator   c. antagonist

3. The protagonist is _____.

    a. the main/central character, sometimes called the hero
    b. the character who opposes the main character, typically creating the conflict
    c. the voice used to tell the story

4. A person or animal who takes part in the action of a literary work is a _____.

    a. character   b. narrator   c. protagonist

5. The time and location in which the story takes place is the _____.

    a. point of view   b. setting   c. theme

6. The antagonist is _____.

    a. the main/central character, sometimes called the hero
    b. the character who opposes the main character, typically creating the conflict

7. The theme of a novel is _____.

    a. the struggle between characters   b. the main idea; the point of the story

8. The highest point of suspense or interest is the _____.

    a. rising action   b. resolution   c. climax

9. A character who shows many different traits and faults is known as _____.

    a. simple   b. round   c. dynamic

10. The end of the central conflict is the _____.

    a. resolution   b. denouement   c. falling action

Lesson 103: Literary Analysis

Here's your next writing project. You'll be doing a literary analysis project for *Emma*. You will be doing the research, reading the novel, and writing the analysis. You will not be turning anything in until you finish the project.

- Make a literary analysis project: power point, sway, etc. OR write a paper or oral presentation to give.

- Some potential topics for your presentation might include:
  - Theme of your novel (meaning and evidence throughout the story)
  - Symbolism in the novel (instances and meanings)
  - Character analysis (motives of character, appearance, etc. and how they are all tied together and to the story)
  - Comparison/contrast between two character (protagonist/antagonist relationship)
  - Setting of your novel (how the author uses the setting to reach the reader and impact the plot)
  - Conflict in your novel (what is it, who is involved, what makes it important)
  - The history of your novel (why it is important to the story and how the author uses it)

- **Requirements for the Project**
  - 10 – 12 Slides
  - Must contain 5 images (with citations)
  - MLA format (include correct page headings on all pages)
  - Must contain in-text citations, correctly formatted
  - Must contain at least five quotes/paraphrases: two from your novel and three from outside sources
  - Title Slide with MLA Header & Works Cited Slide
  - A minimum of five sources for your presentation including the novel. So you can count your novel as one source, and then find four more outside sources. You may have no more than three websites for your sources. Use books, journal articles, etc.
  - If you don't do a Power Point, these will be a little different for you, but this will give you the idea of what you need. Do include images no matter what you choose to do.

- **Helpful hints for gathering your research:**
  - Take notes as you read your novel.
  - Write down important or interesting quotes with page numbers.
  - Write down interesting facts in your novel (setting, character actions, plot points, etc.).
  - Develop a potential thesis and look for information to support that as you read.
  - Look for outside sources as you read you novel. Keep a list of these (title, author, location, date, etc.).

Lesson 104: Plurals and Possessives

Read about plurals and possessives.

- Plurals
  - Apostrophes are seldom used to form a plural noun.
    - Incorrect: The Jones's, a family I've known since the 1990's, often come over on Saturday's and Sunday's for a game night.
    - Correct: The Joneses, a family I've known since the 1990s, often come over on Saturdays and Sundays for a game night.
  - The exception to the rule is when certain abbreviations, letters, or words are used as nouns. Unless the apostrophe is needed to avoid confusion, don't use it to form a plural.
    - Jennifer made straight A's this quarter.
    - Mind your p's and q's.

- Possessives
  - Rather than showing plurality, an apostrophe is used to show possession.
    - If a noun is singular, adding possession simply involves adding an apostrophe and *s*.
      - the teacher's pet
      - the lady's purse
    - If a noun is **singular** and ends in an *s* already, different literary authorities give different rules for showing possession.
      - Some say to add an 's anyway.
        - James's car
      - Others say to just add an apostrophe.
        - James' car
      - Either can be considered correct, but be sure to follow an assignment's directions or preferred writing style if one is given.
        - When a noun is singular but in the form of a plural and ends in *s*, simply add an apostrophe to show possession.
          - The United States' weather patterns
          - New Orleans' culture
    - If a noun is **plural** and ends in an *s*, *always* add the apostrophe after the *s* to show possession.
      - the two boys' soccer ball
      - the three rabbits' ears
    - If a noun is plural and doesn't end in an *s*, simply add an apostrophe and *s* to show possession.
      - the men's room
      - the children's book
    - Joint possession (the possession is shared) only requires one apostrophe.
      - Tina Rutherford and Jennifer Appel's book series *Silverwood Sagas*
        - The book series has more than one author.

- Alyssa and Michal's house
  - They both live in the house.
- Individual possession, even when talking about multiple possessors at once, requires an apostrophe for each possessor.
  - North Carolina's and Tennessee's tax structures are very different.
    - Each state has its own tax structure
  - Kennedy's and William's houses are on the same street.
    - They live in different houses

Write the correct forms of the possessive noun.

the one cats tail

_____

the two birds wings

_____

the mens room

_____

the many cars horns

_____

the one trucks wheels

_____

the five girls dresses

_____

Lesson 105: Biography

Your biography is due today. Score it according to the rubric that was given on Lesson 98. Did you get it done? Take off 10 points for every day you're late. Be sure to get your work done on time!

Lesson 106: Irregular Plurals

Lit & Comp II LA

Refresh your memory on these irregular plurals. If you need to refresh your memory on how to form possessive nouns, study Lesson 104. Then take the quiz.

- We make the plural of nouns that end in CH, SH, X, O or SS by adding ES.
    - one dress, two dresses
    - one fox, two foxes
    - one couch, two couches
    - one wish, two wishes
    - one potato, two potatoes

- We make the plural of some nouns that end in F or FE by changing the F or FE to V and adding ES.
    - one leaf, two leaves
    - one knife, two knives

- We make the plural of nouns that end in Y not following a vowel by changing the Y to I and adding ES.
    - one cherry, two cherries
    - one fly, two flies

- We make the plural of some OO nouns by changing the OO to EE.
    - one foot, two feet
    - one goose, two geese
    - one tooth, two teeth

- We make the plural of some nouns that end in US by changing the US to I
    - one cactus, two cacti
    - one nucleus, two nuclei

- We make the plural of some nouns that end with IS by changing the IS to ES
    - one crisis, two crises
    - one parenthesis, two parentheses

- We make the plural of some nouns that end with ON by changing the ON to A
    - phenomenon, two phenomena
    - one criterion, two criteria

- And of course, there are many words that just don't follow a rule.
    - one man, two men
    - one child, two children

- And some words have the same form whether they're singular or plural.
    - one sheep, two sheep
    - one deer, two deer

Lesson 106: Plurals and Possessives Quiz

Read the following story. If the word preceding the blank is correctly written, put a check in the blank. If it's incorrect, put an x in the blank. Check your answers and record your score out of 25.

      The Meier's _____ are a family of four: Mom, Dad, and two girls. The Meiers' _____ favorite vacation spot is Disney World. Disneys' _____ rooms hold up to four people so it work's _____ out perfectly for the Meiers _____. They always drive down to Disney World. The tradition is to stop at McDonald's _____ for a hot breakfast in the early morning hour's _____. Then they drive as far as they can before stopping again. The girls' _____ favorite thing to do on the road is to pop a Disney DVD into their vans' _____ DVD player and plan out what rides they'll visit first. The family's _____ coin stash is always used up by the Florida toll's _____, but it's a small price to pay for family fun. (One time, Mr. Meier forgot to roll down the driver's _____ window and tossed the quarters _____ straight into the glass. His two daughter's _____ laughs lasted for several minutes after that.)

      Once the familys' _____ journey to Disney is complete, next comes the trek to the parks _____. They always start at the Magic Kingdom. As funny as it sounds, the trip on the buses _____ from the hotel is always an exciting part of the vacation for the Meier girls. The smell of the diesel fuel and the hissing of the brake's _____ are quintessential Disney sights and smells for them. Upon arrival at the Magic Kingdom, the family heads straight for Main Streets' _____ Confectionery for some sweet treats. The girls usually order childrens' _____ sizes because they're still such large servings. Besides _____, they don't want to be too full when they finally get to ride the roller coaster's _____.

      After a long day in the Magic Kingdom of riding rides and indulging in theme park treats, the family likes to watch the fireworks _____ show. Set to various clips of Disney music, the booming explosions light up the night sky while lightly illuminating each of the Meiers' _____ happy faces. With happy hearts and exhausted feet_____, the family returns to wait for the bus to take them back to their hotel, eager for a night of restful sleep before they start it all over again in the morning.

Read about story elements.

Here's our plot diagram from earlier in the course.

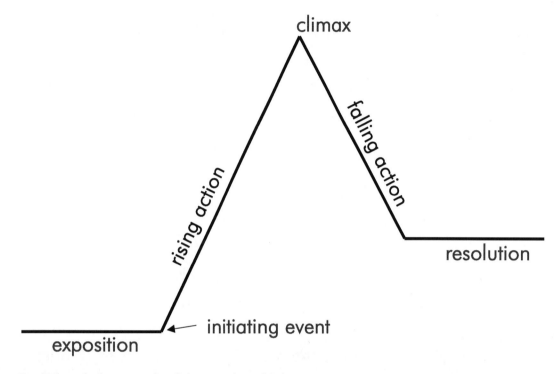

Let's break down each of these points further.

- The beginning of a story usually includes the exposition and the conflict.
  - The **exposition** is the introduction of the story and includes things like the characters' names, the setting, etc.
  - The **conflict** is the main problem that drives the plot of the story, usually introduced by an initiating event in the beginning of the story.

- The middle of the story usually includes the rising action and the climax (though the climax is often closer to the end of the story as well).
  - The **rising action** is the events that lead to the climax, including character development and events that create suspense and tension.
  - The **climax** is usually the most exciting part of the story, the part the preceding action points to, and the turning point for the protagonist.

- The end of the story usually includes the falling action and the resolution.
  - The **falling action** is what happens as a result of the climax. It wraps up the plot points, answers questions, etc.
  - The **resolution** is the completion of the story. It can be happy, sad, confusing, frustrating, etc.

- Here's a sample plot diagram for a hopefully familiar story, *The Three Little Pigs*.

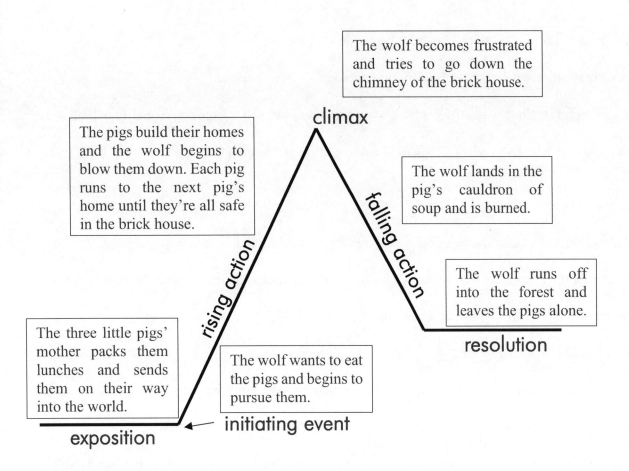

The wolf becomes frustrated and tries to go down the chimney of the brick house.

climax

The pigs build their homes and the wolf begins to blow them down. Each pig runs to the next pig's home until they're all safe in the brick house.

The wolf lands in the pig's cauldron of soup and is burned.

rising action

falling action

The wolf runs off into the forest and leaves the pigs alone.

The three little pigs' mother packs them lunches and sends them on their way into the world.

The wolf wants to eat the pigs and begins to pursue them.

resolution

exposition

initiating event

Review this short story terminology from earlier in the course.

plot: the sequence of events in a story

setting: the time and place where a story takes place

exposition: the beginning of a story that introduces the characters, setting, and basis of the plot

conflict: a problem between a character and another person or force

internal conflict: a struggle inside a character's mind

external conflict: a struggle between a character and someone or something outside of the character

climax: the turning point in a story

rising action: events leading up to the climax

falling action: events following the climax that lead to the resolution

resolution/denouement: the end of a story where the conflict is solved or the outcome of the conflict is seen

character: a person (or an animal) in a literary work

characterization: the process of revealing the personality of a character

direct characterization: when the reader knows directly what a character's personality is like

indirect characterization: when a character's personality is revealed through actions or hints rather than directly

dynamic character: a changing character – one who grows and learns as the story goes on

flat character: a character the reader doesn't know very well or that isn't very developed

static character: a character that remains steady and does not change throughout the story

round character: a fully-developed character about whom the reader knows much

protagonist: the main character

antagonist: the character who works against the protagonist; often the "bad guy" or source of conflict

verbal irony: often portrayed as sarcasm; what is said is opposite of what is meant.

dramatic irony: type of irony in which facts or events are hidden from a character but known to the reader, audience, and/or other characters.

situational irony: when what happens is very different from what was expected

theme: the main idea or meaning of a text

narrator: the person or character who tells the story

point of view: the perspective from which a story is told

figurative language: language that uses figures of speech and can't be taken literally

imagery: descriptive language that appeals to the five senses

symbol: something that stands for something else

suspense: angst or uncertainty the reader feels about what is going to happen next

foreshadowing: hints and clues that suggest what will happen later in the story

Lesson 107: Story Elements Crossword

Solve the crossword puzzle. There are no spaces between words.

Across:
2. the structure used to break down and display story elements
3. this introduces the characters and the conflicts in the story
7. the feeling conveyed to readers by events, characters, setting, etc. in a story
8. events that unfold after the exposition; conflicts progress leading up to the climax

Down:
1. action begins to wrap up; concluding events
4. the ending of the story; loose ends are tied up here
5. another name for resolution
6. the turning point; point of maximum interest or highest tension of the story

Lesson 109: (no LA for Lesson 108) Short Story

Create a character for a short story. Describe him or her in as much detail as possible. Write not only what he looks like but what he sounds like, what he likes to do, what he says all the time, what his strengths and weaknesses are, what makes him mad, what makes him laugh, what intrigues him, what confuses him… Include how you make this a dynamic character. How would this character change over time?

Lesson 110: Short Story

Create a setting for your short story. What's the main setting (time and big location)? Is there more than one minor location (in the house, at the piano recital…)? Use as much detail as possible.

Complete this diagram of the story "A Hunger Artist." Then create an antagonist and conflict for your story. Know everything about it.

Climax:
_____
_____
_____
_____

Complication/Incident:
_____
_____
_____
_____

climax

Falling Action:
_____
_____
_____
_____

Complication/Incident:
_____
_____
_____
_____

falling action

rising action

resolution

Resolution:
_____
_____
_____
_____

exposition

initiating event

Exposition:
_____
_____
_____

Characters:
_____
_____
_____

Setting:
_____

Conflict:
Protagonist
_____
vs.
Antagonist
_____

Situation:
_____
_____
_____

Lesson 112: Short Story

Now complete a plot diagram for your own short story.

Climax:
_____
_____
_____
_____

Complication/Incident:
_____
_____
_____
_____

climax

Falling Action:
_____
_____
_____
_____

Complication/Incident:
_____
_____
_____
_____

rising action

falling action

resolution

Resolution:
_____
_____
_____
_____
_____

exposition

initiating event

Exposition:
_____
_____
_____

Characters:
_____
_____
_____

Setting:
_____
_____

Conflict:
Protagonist

vs.

Antagonist

Situation:
_____
_____
_____
_____
_____

Start writing your short story. It's due on Lesson 116. Write and edit. When you plan out how to manage your time, you should be editing it on Lesson 115. You can read over it again on Lesson 116, but you should never plan to still be working on an assignment the day it's due. You want to be prepared!

Here is the rubric for your short story.

Total points possible = 50 points

1. Ideas/Organization/Content—20 points
   - Setting, characters, and plot are fully fleshed out, vibrant, and connected
   - Flow of action is logical and deliberate
   - Uses multiple subplots (if appropriate)
   - Plot is original/creative/imaginative
   - Uses symbolism or subtext
   - Ending is effective, fitting, and provides a sense of completion

2. Style/Voice—15 points
   - Vivid and imaginative descriptive details are present
   - Writing reflects a unique, consistent personal voice
   - Writing (when appropriate) incorporates/weaves/experiments with different styles

3. Word Choice/Sentence Fluency—10 points
   - Word choice is inventive, sophisticated, and appropriate for work
   - Word choice is consciously appropriate and deliberate for character
   - Sentences read smoothly making it easy to decipher meaning
   - Sentence structure is varied and complex
   - Sentence structure is deliberately manipulated in a sophisticated manner to affect style
   - Dialogue (when present) is effective/appropriate/believable

4. Conventions—5 points
   - Spelling is correct throughout piece
   - Punctuation is used correctly
   - Punctuation is deliberately manipulated in a sophisticated manner to affect style
   - Format and presentation is correct/professional (Times New Roman, size 12, double-spaced)

Take the quiz and record your score on your grade sheet.

1. In "A Hunger Artist," the _____ in this story symbolizes the hunger artist's separation from society.

    a. paintbrush
    b. cage
    c. artist

2. What is the maximum fasting limit the impresario will allow for the hunger artist?

    a. 40 days
    b. 10 days
    c. 30 days

3. How does the hunger artist die?

    a. He dies from loneliness.
    b. He dies from starvation in a cage with little notice.
    c. He dies at the hands of another artist.

4. What takes the place of the hunger artist in the cage?

    a. lion
    b. tiger
    c. panther

Lesson 114: Literary Analysis

Remember to be thinking about your analysis paper (see Lesson 103 for the assignment).

- o Theme of your novel (meaning and evidence throughout the story)
- o Symbolism in the novel (instances and meanings)
- o Character analysis (motives of character, appearance, etc., and how they are all tied together and to the story)
- o Comparison/contrast between two characters (protagonist/antagonist relationship)
- o Setting of your novel (how the author uses the setting to reach the reader and impact the plot)
- o Conflict in your novel (what is it, who is involved, what makes it important)
- o The history of your novel (why it is important to the story and how the author uses it)

Don't forget about your short story assignment.

Lesson 115: Short Story Terms Quiz

Take this short story terms quiz. Record your score out of 6 (potential for extra credit).

character	characterization	direct characterization
dynamic character	flat character	indirect characterization
narrative	round character	short story	static character

A fully-developed character about whom the reader knows much

_____

when a character's personality is revealed through actions or hints

_____

a character the reader doesn't know very well/isn't very developed

_____

the process of revealing a character's personality

_____

a narrative that's typically ten to twenty pages

_____

a changing character – one who grows and learns as the story goes on

_____

a literary work that tells a story

_____

a person or animal in a literary work

_____

a character that remains steady and does not change throughout the story

_____

when the reader knows what a character's personality is like

_____

- Score your short story using the rubric found in Lesson 113. Record it on your grade sheet.
- Now give your short story to your peer editing partner, or at least someone who can read it and give feedback. Send along the grading rubric.
  - Ideally, your peer editing partner is someone in your same grade. They don't have to use Easy Peasy. If you can't find someone like that among your family and friends, then ask someone older than you to read your essay and give you a grade.
- When you get your feedback score, divide it in half and record it.
- Fix up your story based on the feedback. Re-score your story and record it.

Read about your next assignment, your short story newspaper project. For this project, you will put together a newspaper that covers the stories you read in this unit.

- Articles for your Newspaper
  - You will write six articles for your paper. There should be three for each story we read in this unit. You can choose from the article types below, however, you can only write one of each type of article:
    - News Feature Story/Cover Story (could have up to two of these)
    - Opinion article
    - Horoscope
    - Dear Abby letter
    - Obituary
    - Sales/Help Wanted
    - Entertainment
    - Sports
    - Travel
    - Business
    - Outdoor Living
    - "To Do"
    - Comic Strip
  - You can choose any six of these article types, but the article must deal with and contain details from the short stories:
    - "The Adventure of the Noble Bachelor"
    - "A Hunger Artist"
  - Be sure to include facts from your story, while using creativity. For instance, you might use story details to write a horoscope for any of the characters in these selections. You could also create a help wanted ad geared to one of the characters. For instance, the help wanted ad might be for a hunger artist that the main character of that story could fill. Whichever pieces you choose to write, you must have at least two multi-paragraph articles. You must choose at least two lengthy stories to write (2-3 paragraphs). The others can fill in as you choose.
  - Don't forget to create a title for your newspaper, along with page numbers, section headings, etc.

- Pictures for your Newspaper
  - You will also need to include at least two images in your newspaper. These should be pictures that represent aspects of the story you are writing about for the paper. The pictures can be from other sources, but remember that you must cite where you found the picture. Pixabay is a good site for stock/free domain images.

- Here is your rubric for this assignment:

Total points possible = 125

1. 15 points: Article #1:
   1. 10 points: accuracy of supporting details
   2. 5 points: correct spelling, grammar, punctuation, etc.

2. 15 points: Article #2:
   1. 10 points: accuracy of supporting details
   2. 5 points: correct spelling, grammar, punctuation, etc.

3. 15 points: Article #3
   1. 10 points: accuracy of supporting details
   2. 5 points: correct spelling, grammar, punctuation, etc.

4. 15 points: Article #4
   1. 10 points: accuracy of supporting details
   2. 5 points: correct spelling, grammar, punctuation, etc.

5. 15 points: Article #5
   1. 10 points: accuracy of supporting details
   2. 5 points: correct spelling, grammar, punctuation, etc.

6. 15 points: Article #6
   1. 10 points: accuracy of supporting details
   2. 5 points: correct spelling, grammar, punctuation, etc.

7. 15 points: Appropriate Images (minimum two)
   - connected to story
   - appropriate for content

8. 10 points: Overall formatting and design

9. 5 points: Newspaper Title

10. 5 points: Section Headlines

- This is due on Lesson 121. Make sure you leave time for editing layout and adding photos!

Lesson 117: Newspaper Project

Work on your newspaper project. See Lesson 116 for the assignment directions and rubric.

Lesson 118: Newspaper Project

Work on your newspaper project. See Lesson 116 for the assignment directions and rubric.

Lesson 119: Newspaper Project

Work on your newspaper project. See Lesson 116 for the assignment directions and rubric.

Lesson 120: Newspaper Project

Work on your newspaper project. See Lesson 116 for the assignment directions and rubric.

Lesson 121: Newspaper Project

Score your newspaper according to the rubric on Lesson 116. Record your score. Take off 10 points for every day that it is late. You have to turn your work in on time!

Lesson 122: Sentence Structures

Review the types of sentence structures. Then take the quiz on the next page.

- Simple sentences
  - Consist of one independent verb clause (a subject and predicate)
  - The subjects are in bold and the predicates are in italics:
    - **The leaves on the trees** *are blowing*.
    - **The boy** *chased after the ball*.
    - **Running** *is exhausting to me*.

- Compound sentences
  - Consist of two or more independent verb clauses joined by a coordinating conjunction.
  - Each verb clause is in bold and the each coordinating conjunction is in italics.
    - **Michael shot the basketball,** *and* **he won the game.**
    - **The movie was rated R,** *so* **we opted to skip it.**
  - The verb clauses can also be joined by a correlating and coordinating conjunction pair.
  - The correlating conjunctions are underlined.
    - <u>Either</u> **you should stop complaining** *or* **you should walk away.**
    - <u>Both</u> **the rain let up** *and* **the sun came out.**

- Complex sentences
  - Consist of one independent verb clause and one or more dependent adverb clause
    - Adverb clause: dependent clause using a subordinating conjunction
  - Each adverb clause is bold and the verb clauses are in italics.
    - **Because of my headache,** *we had to miss the parade*.
    - *I will make it up to you* **after the headache subsides.**
    - *Once the headaches subsides*, **we can go out to dinner** *before it's time for bed*.

- Compound-complex sentences
  - Consist of two or more independent verb clauses and one or more adverb clauses.
    - A combination of compound and complex sentences.
  - The verb clauses are bold, the adverb clauses are italicized, and the coordinating conjunctions are underlined.
    - *Unless I tell you otherwise*, **I don't want to wake up early**, <u>so</u> **please let me sleep.**
    - **Let's go to the store** *before the rain comes*, <u>and</u> **then let's visit the post office.**

Lesson 122: Sentence Structures

Choose whether each sentence below is simple, compound, or complex. Check your answers and record your score.

1. My brother likes grape jelly, and my sister likes strawberry jelly.
    a. simple sentence   b. compound sentence   c. complex sentence

2. An independent clause connected to a dependent clause makes a ___.
    a. simple sentence   b. compound sentence   c. complex sentence

3. The sky looks nasty, so I'd better grab my raincoat.
    a. simple sentence   b. compound sentence   c. complex sentence

4. While his mom napped, Justin cleaned the kitchen.
    a. simple sentence   b. compound sentence   c. complex sentence

5. Bryce and Bristol read a book together all afternoon.
    a. simple sentence   b. compound sentence   c. complex sentence

6. Mom could not find the car keys although she searched the whole house.
    a. simple sentence   b. compound sentence   c. complex sentence

7. An independent clause that stands alone is a _____.
    a. simple sentence   b. compound sentence   c. complex sentence

8. Two independent clauses connected to each other with a conjunction
    a. simple sentence   b. compound sentence   c. complex sentence

9. The sponsor of the sporting event plastered their logo on every surface.
    a. simple sentence   b. compound sentence   c. complex sentence

10. The song played on the radio before we arrived at the concert.
    a. simple sentence   b. compound sentence   c. complex sentence

Lesson 123: Poetic Devices

Identify which poetic device is being used in each example. Your choices are in the word box (some words are used more than once).

alliteration	hyperbole	idiom	metaphor
onomatopoeia	personification	rhyme	simile

The wind bit my nose as it roared.   _____

The sweet, silly sisters scaled the stairs.   _____

Your room is a pigsty!   _____

Tick tock goes the clock.   _____

A fat cat sat on my hat.   _____

It's raining cats and dogs today.   _____

Her skin was like silky milk chocolate.   _____

That was the easiest question in the world.   _____

Time marches on, despite our objections.   _____

I'm so hungry I could eat a horse!   _____

The snow was a blanket covering the ground.   _____

I think I bit off more than I can chew.   _____

Her hands were as cold as ice.   _____

Lesson 124: Descriptive Writing

Descriptive writing is used to create a picture in your reader's mind by describing the people, places, and things you are writing about in vivid detail.

- Good descriptive writing will appeal to all five senses, allowing the reader to see, hear, touch, smell, and taste the story. They should be able to feel what the characters or writer are feeling.
    - o Not descriptive: My favorite part of the trip was riding the alpine coaster.
    - o Descriptive: The highlight of my vacation was experiencing the adrenaline rush of zooming through the crisp mountain air on the alpine coaster as the trees flew by like green blobs and the wind whipped my hair and burned my nostrils.

- Good descriptive writing will establish a mood.
    - o Not descriptive: I liked when my mom read to me as a child.
    - o Descriptive: I remember many cozy nights snuggled under the blankets in front of a crackling fire as my mom read to me with her soothing voice.

- Good descriptive writing will use vivid language instead of vague language, utilizing strong verbs and expressive adjectives.
    - o Not descriptive: The beach was crowded.
    - o Descriptive: The bevy of humanity that flocked to the beach for the holiday weekend made it difficult to find a spare scrap of sand on which to set up camp.

- Good descriptive writing will have varied sentence structure and varied subject/verb placement within sentences. Combining shorter sentences is one way to achieve this.
    - o Similar structure: Her stomach grumbled. She reached for the bag of chips without looking. She knocked her water cup to the floor.
    - o Combined as one sentence: Absentmindedly reaching for the bag of chips as her stomach grumbled, she heard the sound of splashing water as her water cup tumbled to the floor.

- Good descriptive writing shows instead of telling.
    - o Telling: I was nervous.
    - o Showing: My heart rate elevated as drops of perspiration beaded on my forehead.

- Good descriptive writing will be well-organized either chronologically, spatially, or otherwise.
    - o Don't make your reader work to make sense of your writing.

- Good descriptive writing will utilize figurative language. We've discussed the following terms before:
    - o Alliteration – repeated consonant sounds at the beginning of words
        - ▪ Peter Piper picked a peck of pickled peppers.
    - o Assonance – resembling sounds in words or syllables
        - ▪ Try to light the fire.

- o Hyperbole – exaggeration
  - ▪ My shoes are killing me.
- o Idiom – words that have a meaning established by usage that doesn't make sense with the individual words used
  - ▪ I'm feeling under the weather.
- o Metaphor – a comparison between two unlike things that suggests they are similar
  - ▪ All the world is a stage.
- o Onomatopoeia – words that sound like what they are
  - ▪ Buzz, pop, ding
- o Personification – giving human qualities to something nonhuman
  - ▪ The chair groaned under the weight of the pair sitting in it.
- o Simile – a comparison that uses like or as
  - ▪ Her hair was like golden rays of the sun streaming down her back.
- o AVOID clichés – words or phrases that have become overly familiar or common.
  - ▪ Once upon a time; they lived happily ever after; in the nick of time

- Things to think about when attempting a descriptive writing project:
  - o What/who are you wanting to describe?
  - o Why do you want to describe it/them?
  - o What qualities do you want to focus on?
    - ▪ Do you want people to know what your uncle looked like or that he was kind? The answer will help you narrow your descriptive focus.
  - o How can you appeal to the five senses? What sights, sounds, smells, textures, and tastes can you "show, not tell"?
  - o How can you convey emotion and develop a mood?

- Practice descriptive writing with the exercises on the next page.

Lesson 124: Descriptive Writing

Complete these descriptive writing exercises.

Write a simile.

_____

_____

Write a metaphor.

_____

_____

Rewrite these clichés. How could you express the same thing in a new way?

The apple doesn't fall far from the tree.

_____

She's as sharp as a tack.

_____

Ignorance is bliss.

_____

Look around your room. Write the best descriptive sentence you can about something in the room where you are. Use at least one poetic device.

_____

_____

_____

_____

Refresh your memory on these poetry terms.

alliteration: the repetition of words that have the same first consonant sounds next to or close to each other

allusion: an indirect reference to something such as another work of literature, a historical event, biblical story, mythical character, etc.

blank verse: un-rhyming verse written in iambic pentameter

consonance: repetitive sounds produced by consonants within a sentence or phrase

descriptive essay: an essay that uses similes, metaphors, and other figurative language to illustrate something in a way the reader can see, feel, or hear what is being written

end rhyme: rhymes that have the same ending sounds

feet: the combination of stressed and unstressed syllables

figurative language: uses figures of speech to be more effective, persuasive, and impactful

heroic couplet: two rhymed lines in iambic pentameter

hyperbole: a figure of speech that is an extreme exaggeration in order to create emphasis

iambic pentameter: an iamb is a type of foot consisting of one stressed syllable and one unstressed syllable (such as the word "remark"). "Pent" means five. So a line of iambic pentameter consists of five iambs – five sets of unstressed syllables followed by stressed syllables.

internal rhyme: rhymes that occur within a line of poetry

metaphor: a figure of speech that makes a direct comparison and shows similarities between two different things without using "like" or "as"

meter: a unit of rhythm in poetry; the pattern of the beats. It is also called a foot. Each foot has a certain number of syllables in it, usually two or three syllables. The difference in types of meter is which syllables are accented and which are not.

oxymoron: a figure of speech in which two opposite ideas are joined to create an effect

personification: a figure of speech in which a thing, an idea, or an animal is given human attributes

refrain: a repeated part of a poem, particularly at the end of a stanza, or between stanzas

repetition: a literary device that repeats the same words or phrases a few times to make an idea clearer

rhyme: two or more words or phrases that end in the same sound

Shakespearean sonnet: the sonnet form used by Shakespeare, composed of three quatrains and a terminal couplet in iambic pentameter with the rhyme pattern abab cdcd efef gg

slant rhyme: rhymes that are close, but not exact

simile: a figure of speech that makes a comparison and shows similarities between two different things by using "like" or "as"

sonnet: a poem of fourteen lines using any number of formal rhyme schemes; in English – typically having ten syllables per line

stanza: a group of lines in a poem

symbol: an object or idea that represents or stands for something else – especially a material object having a deeper meaning

Read about analyzing poetry.

- One way to better understand poetry is by analyzing the elements that make up a good poem. Poems are written in either closed or open form. Closed form poems are written in specific patterns, using meter, line length, and line groupings called stanzas. Open form poems, often still referred to as "free verse" poems, do not use regular rhythmic patterns (i.e., metric feet), are usually unrhymed, have varying line lengths, and have no set line groupings. Remember that you are looking for relationships between the formal devices of poetry, like word choice, metric pattern, and metaphor and the poem's subject. A thorough investigation of the elements of a poem helps the reader to better understand the poem.

- The following list is a guide providing characteristics to look for when analyzing poetry.

1. DETERMINE THE SUBJECT OF THE POEM
- Paraphrase/summarize the poem; what is it about?
- Does the poem address a social, psychological, historical, or mythical phenomenon?

2. IDENTIFY THE POEM'S NARRATOR
- Who is speaking?
- To whom?
- Under what circumstances? Identify the setting.

3. NOTE THE DICTION (WORD CHOICE) OF THE POET
- Be sure to look up all unfamiliar words in a dictionary.
- What are the words' denotations and connotations?
- Is the poem free of clichés?
- How does the diction contribute to or detract from the poem?

4. DETERMINE THE TONE OF THE POEM
- Is the poem serious? Ironic? Satiric? Contemplative? Ambiguous?
- Point out words that set the tone.
- Determine whether the tone changes within the poem.

5. DETERMINE THE RHYTHMICAL DEVICES USED BY THE POET
- What is the basic metrical pattern? Line length?
- What is the length of the stanza?
- What is the rhyme scheme? End rhyme? Internal rhyme?
- Does the poet employ any other metrical device?
- What form does the poem take? Open or closed?

6. NOTE THE USE OF OTHER LITERACY DEVICES
- What allusions does the poem contain?
- Listen to the sounds in the poem. Make note of assonance, alliteration, and onomatopoeia.
- Does the poet use figurative language, such as metaphor, simile, symbolism, imagery, irony, personification, antithesis, hyperbole, metonymy, synecdoche, allegory, paradox, understatement, or overstatement?
- Are there any examples of synecdoche or metonymy?
- Note the use, or absence, of punctuation.
- Titles are important. Is the title the best the writer could have chosen? What would be a better title for the work? Why?

7. DETERMINE THE VALUES OF THE POEM
- Does the poet succeed in recreating his experiences within the reader? How?
- Is the experience intensely felt by the reader?
- Does the poem succeed in sharpening the reader's awareness of something significant?

- Lines in poetry are generally made up of metrical feet. Metrical feet (the combination of accented and unaccented syllables) are usually one of the following:

1. TWO –SYLLABLE FEET

- **Iamb**: consists of light stress followed by a heavy stress. **Example: the winds**
- **Trochee**: a heavy stress followed by a light stress. **Example: flower**
- **Spondee**: Two successive, equally heavy stresses. **Example: men's eyes**
- **Pyrric**: two successive unstressed syllables. **Example: the soft**

2. THREE-SYLLABLE FEET

- **Anapest**: Two light stresses followed by a heavy stress: Example: **early light**
- **Dactyl**: A heavy stress followed by two lights. **Example: this is the**

- The combination of metrical feet determines a poem's **meter**. The types of meter are:

A. **Dimeter**: a line of two two-syllable feet
B. **Trimeter**: a line of three feet
C. **Tetrameter**: a four-foot line
D. **Pentameter**: a line of five feet
E. **Hexameter**: a six-foot line
F. **Heptameter**: a seven-foot line
G. **Octameter**: eight feet.

(Lesson from GAVL, creative commons 3.0 [https://creativecommons.org/licenses/by/3.0/], http://cms.gavirtualschool.org/Shared/Language%20Arts/10thLitComp/09_PoetryTwo/analyzing_poetry.pdf)

- Read these poems once to get the mood, the feeling of them. Do you recognize a theme?

The Swing
By Robert Louis Stevenson

How do you like to go up in a swing,
  Up in the air so blue?
Oh, I do think it the pleasantest thing
  Ever a child can do!

Up in the air and over the wall,
  Till I can see so wide,
Rivers and trees and cattle and all
  Over the countryside—

Till I look down on the garden green,
  Down on the roof so brown—
Up in the air I go flying again,
  Up in the air and down!

Playgrounds
By Laurence Alma-Tadema

In summer I am very glad
We children are so small,
For we can see a thousand things
That men can't see at all.

They don't know much about the moss
And all the stones they pass:
They never lie and play among
The forests in the grass:

They walk about a long way off;
And, when we're at the sea,
Let father stoop as best he can
He can't find things like me.

But, when the snow is on the ground
And all the puddles freeze,
I wish that I were very tall,
High up above the trees.

- Read them again with a pencil in hand and mark all of the figurative language you can identify.

- Write a paragraph (or poem about ten lines long) describing the following scene. Use figurative language. If you'd prefer to look at a color version, you can find one in the online course or at the Wikimedia link of attribution below the photo.

Lesson 126: Descriptive Writing

Complete this descriptive writing assignment. Grade it according to the rubric and record your score.

- Use one of the pictures that follow these instructions or a picture of your favorite park, your car, or even your room.

- First you will write a descriptive paragraph about the picture you choose. It should be 12-14 sentences in length. It should also contain at least FIVE examples of figurative language. You may repeat ONE figurative language item. For instance, you might include simile, metaphor, hyperbole, and imagery. For your fifth item, you could repeat one of those or choose a new one. You can always use more than FIVE examples, but FIVE is the minimum.

- Next, you will identify the figurative language in your descriptive paragraph. You will do this below the completed paragraph. Simply give the figurative language term and then give the example from your writing.

- **Example:** Alliteration – The dreary, dusty driveway led many friends and family to our home. (Do this for each of your five examples… and more, if you have them).

Choose one of these photos or one of your own. There are color photos in the online assignment if you prefer to use one of those:

Children sliding

Factory at sunset

Family eating dinner

Marines praying

Oil spill

Score your assignment according to this rubric.

Total points possible = 50

1. 5 points: Correct Length (12-14 sentences)

2. 10 points: Correct spelling/grammar/punctuation

3. 5 points each for:
    1. Figurative Language #1: _____
    2. Figurative Language #2: _____
    3. Figurative Language #3:_____
    4. Figurative Language #4: _____
    5. Figurative Language #5:_____

4. 10 points: Overall descriptive effect

Lesson 127: Poem Assignment

Complete this poem assignment.

Now it is time to turn your descriptive paragraph into a poem. Using the same picture and details from your descriptive writing, compose a poem describing your picture. You must include at least THREE examples of figurative language in your poem. These can be similar examples. You can use the same terms, but you should try to vary the way you use them. So, you might use alliteration again, but you would use different words to do this.

Your poem should be at least TEN lines long. They can rhyme, but they do not have to rhyme. They can be short fragments, or full sentences.

Remember that both your descriptive paragraph and your poem should be bursting with descriptive detail. Your goal is to paint a picture using words. An artist would not just use "red." He or she might use burnt sienna, coral red, brick red, etc., in order to show the various elements of the work. Likewise, a writer would not use "pretty" to describe something. He or she might use words like radiant, luminous, breathtaking, etc. Do the same in your writing. Show us; don't tell us!

Score your assignment according to this rubric.

Total points possible = 50

1. 10 points: Correct Length (10 lines)

2. 10 points: Correct spelling/grammar/punctuation

3. 5 points each for:
   1. Figurative Language #1: _____
   2. Figurative Language #2: _____
   3. Figurative Language #3: _____

4. 15 points: Overall descriptive effect

Lesson 128: Poetic Devices Crossword

Complete the crossword puzzle.

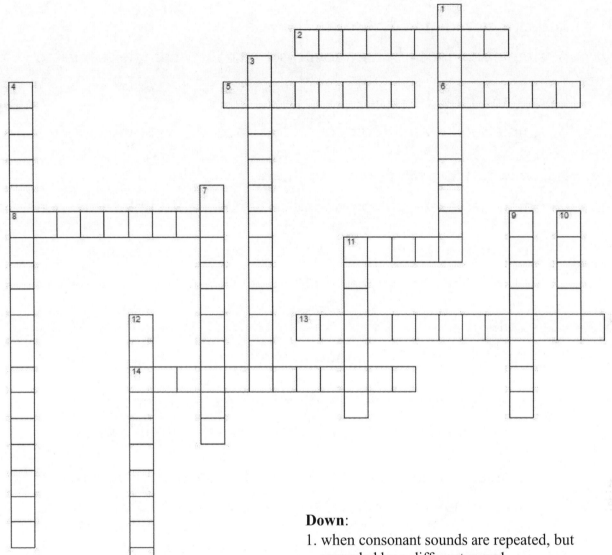

Across:
2. an extreme exaggeration to make a point
5. rhymes that have the same ending sounds (ex. stay and way)
6. a comparison between two things using "like" or "as"
8. repetition of vowel sounds
11. repetition of the end sounds of words
13. two rhymed lines in iambic pentameter
14. repetition of beginning consonant sounds

Down:
1. when consonant sounds are repeated, but preceded by a different vowel
3. rhymes that occur within a line of poetry
4. any type of writing that takes the words beyond their literal meaning
7. when a word, phrase, line, or stanza is repeated in a poem
9. a comparison between two unlike things, saying one thing IS another
10. the main idea in a work of literature
11. a repeated part of a poem, particularly at the end of a stanza, or between stanzas
12. rhyme that are close, but not exact

Lesson 128: Sentence Types Quiz

Choose whether each sentence below is simple, compound, or complex.

1. Rebecca stayed in bed because she was sick.

    b. simple sentence   b. compound sentence   c. complex sentence

2. Please hand me the remote.

    b. simple sentence   b. compound sentence   c. complex sentence

3. Kaitlyn wants to play a game, so I'm going to play one with her.

    b. simple sentence   b. compound sentence   c. complex sentence

4. If you want to have dessert, you'll have to finish your dinner.

    b. simple sentence   b. compound sentence   c. complex sentence

5. Look out!

    b. simple sentence   b. compound sentence   c. complex sentence

6. Although we tried our best, we didn't win the three-legged race.

    b. simple sentence   b. compound sentence   c. complex sentence

7. Traci wants to come over, but she hasn't finished her homework.

    b. simple sentence   b. compound sentence   c. complex sentence

8. When Chase grows up, he wants to be an engineer.

    b. simple sentence   b. compound sentence   c. complex sentence

9. The light turned red before we got through the intersection.

    b. simple sentence   b. compound sentence   c. complex sentence

10. Natalie wants a pet bunny, but she doesn't know how to care for it.

    b. simple sentence   b. compound sentence   c. complex sentence

Lesson 128: Poetry Notebook Project Lit & Comp II LA

Read about your next project. It is due on Lesson 132. Make sure you leave time for making the media part of your project. Follow the directions carefully.

- **Multi-Media Poetry Notebook Project**
    - o For this project, you will put together a virtual "notebook" of sorts. You will compile poems that you find and a few poems of your own, and then you will analyze those poems. This notebook will demonstrate your knowledge of the poetic terms we've discussed, as well as your ability to understand poetry as a whole.

- **Section One: Borrowed Poems**
    - o For this section, you will locate THREE poems from various sources and authors.
    - o Each poem must be from a different author. These can be about any topic.
    - o ONE poem per page.
    - o For each poem:
        - ▪ Type the poem on the page.
        - ▪ In paragraph form, give the overall theme of the poem and your thoughts on the poem. Explain the overall meaning and any interesting details you may have found.
        - ▪ In list form, list the poetic devices/figurative language you found in the poem. Give the device name, and then the example.
    - o Insert graphics – You should find a graphic you think best represents the poem on the page. Remember to give credit to the artist/photographer of the graphic! (see MLA rules for citing photos)

- **Section Two: Original Poems**
    - o For this section, you will compose TWO ORIGINAL poems. These must be your original poems.
        - ▪ One of your poems should deal with a topic similar to the poems we read in this unit. (ex. Childhood memories, parks, playgrounds, etc.).
        - ▪ The other poem can be about any topic.
    - o ONE poem per page.
    - o For each poem:
        - ▪ Type the poem on the page
        - ▪ In paragraph form, give your overall goals of the poem (theme, inspiration, etc.), as well as any interesting details.
        - ▪ In list form, list the poetic devices/figurative language used in the poem. Give the device name, and then the example.
        - ▪ Insert graphics – You should find a graphic you think best represents the poem on the page. Remember to give credit to the artist/photographer of the graphic (see MLA rules for citing photos).

- **Section Three: Poetry Glossary**
  - For this section, you will create a glossary of poetic terms. You should have at least 15 terms for this.
    - Seven (7) terms can come from our course.
    - Eight (8) terms should be found elsewhere.
  - You may put multiple terms on each page for this section.
  - For each term:
    - Type the term and the definition.
    - Give an example of the term.

- **Presentation Options:**
  - You have several options for the format for this project.
    - PowerPoint – create a slideshow, insert pictures, and record narration.
    - Prezi – This is an online presentation tool that allows you to create more detailed presentations. You can check it out using the following link: http://prezi.com/learn/
    - Yola – This is a free website hosting service. You could create a free website.

Project Rubric:

- **Section One: Borrowed Poems**
  - Poem 1
    - 5 points for poem with author credit
    - 5 points for explanation/summary/theme
    - 5 points for figurative language identified/explained
  - Poem 2
    - 5 points for poem with author credit
    - 5 points for explanation/summary/theme
    - 5 points for figurative language identified/explained
  - Poem 3
    - 5 points for poem with author credit
    - 5 points for explanation/summary/theme
    - 5 points for figurative language identified/explained

- **Section Two: Original Poems**
  - Poem 1
    - 5 points for original poem written (given topic)
    - 5 points for explanation/summary/theme
    - 5 points for figurative language identified/explained
  - Poem 2
    - 5 points for original poem written (chosen topic)
    - 5 points for explanation/summary/theme
    - 5 points for figurative language identified/explained

- **Section Three: Poetry Terms Glossary**
  - 5 points for 7 terms from course
  - 5 points for 8 terms from outside course
  - 5 points for examples given for each term
  - 5 points for terms correctly identified/explained

- **Overall Presentation:**
  - 5 points for neatness and originality
  - 5 points for graphics present throughout (minimum 5 images with credits)

- **Total Points Possible 105**

(Assignment from GAVL, creative commons 3.0 [https://creativecommons.org/licenses/by/3.0/], http://cms.gavirtualschool.org/Shared/Language%20Arts/10thLitComp/09_PoetryTwo/MultiMediaPoetryNotebook.pdf)

Lesson 129: Poetry Notebook Project
Lit & Comp II LA

Continue to work on your multimedia poetry notebook project.

Lesson 130: Poetry Notebook Project
Lit & Comp II LA

Continue to work on your multimedia poetry notebook project.

Lesson 131: Poetry Notebook Project
Lit & Comp II LA

Continue to work on your multimedia poetry notebook project.

Finish your project and record your score out of 105 according to the rubric. Take off 10 points for every day it's late.

STOP
This is the end of the third quarter. It's time to save some work in your portfolio. You should probably save all of your major written work: the newspaper and the short story. At this point you can total up your scores from the third quarter. Divide the total by the total possible and then multiply by 100 for your grade. (Just ignore decimals.) This is your third quarter grade. At the end of the year, we can add in points for completing the reading and daily assignments, but you should try for an A. Look at where you lost points and think about what you need to do to not lose them again.

Read over these traditional short story terms. Some should be review. Quiz yourself on them and make sure you're familiar with each one.

Fable: A short story that usually is about animals and is intended to teach a lesson.

Fairytale: A type of short story that has magic and good vs. evil characters.

Tall Tale: An exaggerated, unreliable story told for entertainment.

Trickster Tale: A tale that includes a trickster – a clever animal or person who plays tricks on other characters.

Legend: A traditional story sometimes popularly regarded as historical but can't be proven.

Myths: A made up story that explains the existence of a natural phenomenon.

Wisdom Literature: Literature that teaches how to live properly.

Moral: A message or lesson to be learned from a story or play.

Motif: A recurring image, idea, or symbol.

Archetype: A universally known or understood character, situation, or theme.

Villain: An evil character in the story.

Hero: A character admired for good acts.

Setting: The time and place in which a story takes place.

Plot: The series of events that make up a story.

Characters: A person in a novel, story, play, or movie.

Indirect Characterization: When the narrator shows the reader something about the character through the character's actions, things the character says, or things other characters say.

Direct Characterization: When the author specifically reveals traits about the character in a direct, straightforward manner.

Flat Character: A character whose personality can be described as having one or two personality traits and who does not have a lot of importance or depth.

Round Character: A complex character with many personality traits and who does have many characteristics, high importance, and much depth.

Static Character: A character who does not undergo any type of inner change (personality/attitude) throughout the text.

Dynamic Character: A character who does undergo a type of inner change (personality/attitude) throughout the text.

Foil Characters: A character who creates a contrast to a different character in order to highlight particular qualities of the other character (good appears more "good" when evil is present).

Point of View: The perspective from which a story is told.

Theme: The main idea of a piece of writing or work of literature that an author is trying to express to the reader about life or human nature.

Internal Conflict: The psychological or mental struggle within the mind of a literary or dramatic character.

External Conflict: The struggle between a literary or dramatic character and an outside force such as nature or another character.

Protagonist: The main character of a literary work.

Antagonist: A character or force against which another character struggles.

Mood: The attitude the reader has from a text or work of literature.

Tone: The attitude the writer gives off toward a subject.

Symbolism: The use of one object or idea to represent another object or idea.

- Review the rules of subject/verb agreement on the next page. Then take the quiz.

Lesson 142: Subject/Verb Agreement

Remember that subjects and verbs must agree with each other in number (singular or plural). If you need to, review these 9 subject-verb agreement rules. You will have a graded subject-verb agreement quiz following this lesson. You can also review the end of Lesson 46 to help you.

1. A phrase or clause between the subject and verb does not change the number of the subject.
   - The **men** who attended the rally **were** tired.
     - The plural verb **were** agrees with the plural subject **men**, not the singular *rally*.

2. Singular indefinite pronoun subjects take singular verbs and plural indefinite pronoun subjects take plural verbs.
   - Singular indefinite pronouns include: anybody, anyone, anything, each, either, everybody, everyone, everything, neither, no one, nobody, nothing, one, somebody, someone, something.
   - Plural indefinite pronouns include: several, few, both, many
   - Some can be either singular or plural. If the pronoun points to something uncountable, you use a singular verb. If the pronoun points to something countable, you use a plural verb.
     - These pronouns include things like: some, any, none, all, most

3. Compound subjects joined by **and** are always plural.
   - A **bucket** and **shovel** *were* found buried in the snow.
     - The bucket and shovel connect to make a plural necessitating the plural verb *were*.

4. Compound subjects joined by **or** or **nor** require a verb that agrees with the subject that is closest to it.
   - Neither the **teacher** <u>nor</u> the **students** *were* excited for quiz.
     - The plural *were* agrees with the closer subject *students*.
   - Neither the **students** <u>nor</u> the **teacher** *was* excited for the quiz.
     - The singular *was* agrees with the closer subject *teacher*.

5. Subjects and verbs must still agree when they're inverted (the verb comes first).
   - There **is** a **bear** in the tree.
     - *Is* and *bear* are both singular.
   - How **are** the **children** planning to spend the weekend?
     - *Are* and *children* are both plural.

6. Collective nouns such as team, group, crowd, etc. can be singular or plural, depending on if they're acting together (singular) or as individuals (plural).
   - The **class** *is* voting for extra recess.
     - The whole class is acting as one group.
   - Half the **class** *are* voting for extra recess and half *are* voting for longer lunch.

- o The members of the class are not acting as a single group.

7. Titles of single entities such as books, countries, and organizations are always singular.
   - **General Motors** *makes* vehicles.
     - o The singular company takes a singular verb.

8. Plural form subjects with a singular meaning take a singular verb (measles, news, etc.). Plural form subjects with a plural meaning take a plural verb (scissors, pants, etc.). Some plural form subjects can be either so it will depend on meaning (economics, politics, etc.).
   - **Physics** *is* her favorite subject.
     - o **Physics** is a singular subject.
   - The **news** *wasn't* good.
     - o The **news** is a singular thing.
   - The **pants** *are* on the floor.
     - o The word **pants** as a subject always takes a plural verb.
   - The **pair** of pants *is* on the floor.
     - o The subject here is **pair**, taking a singular verb.
   - **Politics** *is* an interesting topic.
     - o **Politics** is a single topic here.
   - The **politics** of the situation *are* complicated.
     - o **Politics** refers to many aspects of the situation here.

9. When a subject and subjective complement disagree in number, the verb agrees with the subject.
   1. My favorite **topic** *is* <u>songs</u> by Steven Curtis Chapman.
      - The singular subject **topic** needs a singular verb *is*, regardless of the plural subjective complement <u>songs</u>.
   2. **Songs** by Steven Curtis Chapman *are* my favorite <u>topic</u>.
      - Here the subject is the plural **songs** and so the verb needs to be plural: *are*.

- Special tip: a prepositional phrase will never contain the subject of a sentence. This can be helpful in determining a sentence's subject.
  - o Neither of those girls… "of those girls" is a prepositional phrase, so "neither" is the singular subject and the verb needs to be singular: … is coming to lunch with us.
  - o Tristan, along with his brothers… "along with his brothers" is a prepositional phrase, so again, the verb needs to be singular: … wants to try out for the soccer team.

- Review each of these rules until you're ready for the graded quiz on the next pages.

Lesson 142: Subject/Verb Agreement Quiz Lit & Comp II LA

Choose the correct **present tense** verb for each sentence. When you're finished, check your answers and record your score out of 25.

1. Each man, woman, and child _____ food and shelter.

    a. will need   b. need   c. needs   d. needed

2. Politics _____ made friends into enemies.

    a. has   b. have   c. will have   d. had

3. Alice's, famous for delicious club sandwiches, _____ developed a new sandwich.

    a. is   b. had   c. have   d. has

4. Every cucumber, zucchini, and pepper from the garden _____ amazing.

    a. tasted   b. has tasted   c. tastes   d. taste

5. All of my favorite foods _____ on sale this week.

    a. is   b. are   c. was   d. were

6. There _____ Stephanie and Ben on their bikes.

    a. went   b. has gone   c. goes   d. go

7. Not only the Andersons but also Lindsay _____ tried the new deli.

    a. will have   b. has   c. have   d. had

8. There _____ more papers to be filed than you think.

    a. was   b. were   c. are   d. is

(continued on next page)

9. Raking leaves into piles taller than me _____ Kim, my hardworking daughter.

    a. is   b. are   c. was   d. were

10. Johnson and Johnson _____ a baby shampoo with a nostalgic smell.

    a. makes   b. make   c. made   d. have made

11. Neither the encyclopedias nor the dictionary _____ the word I'm looking for.

    a. had   b. will have   c. have   d. has

12. Not only the clouds but also the shade_____ it feel colder under the tree.

    a. made   b. make   c. makes   d. will make

13. The jury _____ to adjourn for the day.

    a. are wanting   b. wants   c. wanted   d. want

14. _____ no one except Andy and Bev remember the answer to the riddle?

    a. Has   b. Did   c. Does   d. Do

15. Ten dollars _____ a lot of money to spend on a single lunch.

    a. is   b. are   c. was   d. were

16. The sisters, along with Bradley, _____ to avoid the traffic by leaving early.

    a. hoped   b. will hope   c. hope   d. hopes

17. Neither of my parents _____ attending the meeting.

    a. is   b. are   c. was   d. were

(continued on next page)

18. Here _____ the sandwich and chips you ordered.

    a. is   b. are   c. was   d. were

19. My dog, together with my cat, _____ to lay on the heater vents in the winter.

    a. likes   b. like   c. liked   d. had liked.

20. Each of my brothers _____ a different sport.

    a. enjoys   b. enjoy   c. enjoyed   d. will enjoy

21. On the hill _____ many rocks that slow our biking progress.

    a. is   b. are   c. was   d. were

22. Jessica is one of those girls who _____ long hair.

    a. liked   b. likes   c. like   d. has liked

23. A donut with sprinkles_____ more fun than one without sprinkles.

    a. were   b. was   c. are   d. is

24. There already _____ skaters at the rink.

    a. is   b. are   c. has been   d. had been

25. Measles _____ about two weeks.

    a. will last   b. lasted   c. last   d. lasts

Refresh your memory on these poetry terms. *(Remember to be completing lessons in your Reader and Vocabulary Workbook.)*

Stanza: A group of lines in a poem.

Alliteration: The repetition of words that have the same first consonant sounds either next to each other or close together.

Rhyme: Two or more words or phrases that end in the same sound.

Allusion: A casual or indirect reference to something else such as another work of literature, a historical event, a biblical story, or mythology.

Symbol: An object or idea that represents or stands for something else— especially a material object having a deeper meaning.

Figurative Language: Using figures of speech to be more effective, persuasive and impactful. Figures of speech such as metaphors, similes, allusions go beyond the literal meanings of the words to give the readers visual images.

Hyperbole: A figure of speech that is an extreme exaggeration in order to create emphasis.

Repetition: A literary device that repeats the same words or phrases a few times to make an idea clearer.

Meter: Meter is a unit of rhythm in poetry, the pattern of the beats. It is also called a foot. Each foot has a certain number of syllables in it, usually two or three syllables. The difference in types of meter is which syllables are accented and which are not.

Feet: The combination of stressed and unstressed syllables.

Iambic Pentameter: A specific type of foot is an iamb. A foot is an iamb if it consists of one unstressed syllable followed by a stressed syllable, so the word "remark" is an iamb. "Pent" means five, so a line of iambic pentameter consists of five iambs – five sets of unstressed syllables followed by stressed syllables.

Blank Verse: A literary device defined as un-rhyming verse written in iambic pentameter.

Sonnet: A poem of fourteen lines using any of a number of formal rhyme schemes, in English typically having ten syllables per line.

Shakespearean Sonnet: The sonnet form used by Shakespeare, composed of three quatrains and a terminal couplet in iambic pentameter with the rhyme pattern abab cdcd efef gg.

Simile: A figure of speech that makes a comparison and shows similarities between two different things by using "like" or "as."

Metaphor: A figure of speech that makes a direct comparison and shows similarities between two different things without using "like" or "as."

Personification: A figure of speech in which a thing, an idea or an animal is given human attributes.

Oxymoron: A figure of speech in which two opposite ideas are joined to create an effect.

Descriptive Essay: An essay that uses similes, metaphors, and other figurative language to illustrate something in a way that the reader can see, feel, or hear whatever is being written.

Refresh your memory on prepositional phrases.

- A prepositional phrase begins with a preposition and ends with a noun, pronoun, gerund, or clause (known as the object of the preposition).
    - at church – preposition + noun
    - with her – preposition + pronoun
    - without apologizing – preposition + gerund

- Sometimes there are modifiers that describe the object of the preposition.
    - from my mom – preposition + modifier + noun

- A prepositional phrase functions as an adjective or adverb.
    - If it answers the question *Which one*? it functions as an adjective.
        - The towel **on your bedroom floor** is all wet.
            - Which towel? The one on your bedroom floor.
    - If it answers the questions *How? When?* or *Where?* it functions as an adverb.
        - We need to go to the store **before dark**.
            - When do we need to go to the store? Before dark.

- Note: as a reminder, a prepositional phrase will not ever contain a sentence's subject. This can help you as you're trying to identify the subject of a sentence and figure out if it's plural or singular. We've run into this already in our subject/verb agreement lessons and quizzes.

Take the prepositional phrase quiz on the next page.

Lesson 146: Prepositional Phrase Quiz

Underline the prepositional phrases in each sentence below. Some sentences have more than one prepositional phrase.

1. The neighbors across the street lost their tree in a storm.

2. At the stroke of midnight, I will be thirteen years old.

3. I've met three different Jennifers since Tuesday.

4. My meatball rolled under the table.

5. Before your first day, make sure you know the requirements of the job.

6. It was beyond me why anyone wanted to ride on the spinning rides.

7. We got lost along the way, but we finally found the route to the house.

8. He beat me to the park by running the whole way.

9. There was a massive wind storm during the night.

10. We took a touristy picture outside Buckingham Palace.

11. I was busy all day between cooking and cleaning.

12. When we lined up against the wall, I was behind my brother.

13. Let's not go down that rabbit trail.

14. Do you want to come with me to the library?

15. Did you check beside the computer?

Take this quiz on *Emma*. Record your score out of 10 (potential for extra credit).

1. Emma lives in Hartfield with...

   a. her father and sister   c. her father, sister, and governess

   b. her father   d. her father and mother

2. What does Frank Churchill do for Harriet?

   a. He defends her against Augusta's attacks.

   b. He marries her and she doesn't have to become a governess.

   c. He saves her from gypsies.

   d. He gives her money for a debt.

3. As the novel begins, whom has Emma matched with her neighbor, Mr. Weston?

   a. Isabella, her sister   c. Augusta Hawkins, her acquaintance

   b. Harriet, her friend   d. Miss Taylor, her governess

4. Whom does Mr. Weston think that George Knightly is fond of?

   a. Jane Fairfax   b. Harriet   c. Augusta Hawkins   d. Miss Bates

5. What incident causes George Knightly to think Frank Churchill is a "trifling, silly fellow"?

   a. His excessive flirting with Augusta at the dance

   b. His purchase of a pianoforte

   c. His travelling to London for a haircut

   d. His insistence at having a ball at the Crown Inn

6. When Harriet says she is interested in someone above her station, whom does Emma think she is referring to?

   a. Mr. Knightly   b. Mr. Martin   c. Mr. Churchill   d. Mr. Weston

7. Who says this line: "Better to be without sense than to misapply it as you do"?

   a. Emma   b. Harriet   c. Frank Churchill   d. George Knightly

(continued on next page)

8. Which of the following couples are NOT engaged by the end of the book?

   a. Miss Bates and Mr. Perry

   b. Emma and Mr. Knightly

   c. Harriet and Mr. Martin

9. What does George Knightly do for Harriet?

   a. He saves her from gypsies.

   b. He gives her advice not to marry Robert Martin.

   c. He asks her to dance when Mr. Elton ignores her.

   d. He saves her from her water-surrounded carriage.

10. How does Emma's first match for Harriet end?

    a. Mr. Elton falls in love with Emma and then marries Augusta.

    b. Mr. Elton's family won't give consent.

    c. Augusta shows up and claims she is betrothed to Mr. Elton

    d. Harriet rejects Mr. Elton's pursuit of her.

11. Why is Emma upset when she finds out Harriet has feelings for Mr. Knightly?

    a. Emma wanted Mr. Knightly to marry Jane Fairfax.

    b. Emma loves Mr. Knightly.

    c. Emma had promised Harriet to Mr. Churchill.

    d. Emma doesn't think Mr. Knightly is respectable.

12. Why does Emma not think Robert Martin is a good match for Harriet?

    a. He is not titled.   c. He is not proper enough.

    b. He lives with his family.   d. Mr. Knightly doesn't trust him.

13. For what does George Knightly reprimand Emma?

    a. Her love of dancing   c. Her disrespect of Mrs. Weston's position

    b. The way she treats her father   d. Her rudeness at a picnic to Miss Bates

Write four lines of iambic pentameter. Here are some tips for reading Shakespeare out loud that you can apply to the writing and reading of your lines of iambic pentameter. Then read them to an audience. Record 25 points: 5 points for each line that correctly follows the format, 5 points for delivery if your audience could hear and understand you.

- Shakespearean dialogue is not the same as the writing in a novel or other similar literary work. Since the dialogue is written for performers, everything the actor needs to know is written into the dialogue. You have to get the stress right. (be**gin**, **trum**pet – the bold shows the stress), but here are where other clues are hidden in Shakespeare's writing.
  - Imagery
    - When Shakespeare wrote and performed, there wasn't scenery and lighting like there is today to create the scene. Shakespeare used language to create the moods and scenes that would be portrayed.
      - "I know a bank whereon the wild thyme blows,
        Where oxlips and nodding violet grows," – *A Midsummer Night's Dream*
        - The dialogue paints a picture.
  - Punctuation
    - The punctuation in a Shakespeare play is not used in a formal sense; rather it's used to tell the actor how to deliver each line.
      - Period
        - A period in Shakespeare's writing was the signal for a full stop. It naturally brought the energy of the line to a close.
      - Sporadic commas
        - As in formal writing, commas in Shakespeare's writing cause a natural slight pause in delivery. This can signal a small development, a shift in the character's thought process, etc.
      - Repetition of commas
        - A repetition of commas can help raise the intensity of a line. When Shakespeare used a lot of commas together and evenly spaced, he wanted the actor to emotionally invest in the dialogue and build its intensity rhythmically.
          - "No, no, no life!
            Why should a dog, a horse, a rat have life,
            And thou no breath at all? Thou'it come no more;
            Never, never, never, never, never." – *King Lear*
      - Colon
        - A colon shows that the next line should sound as if it is responding to the line before the colon.
          - "To be, or not to be: that is the question." – *Hamlet*

- It can be tempting to pause at the end of each line of written verse, but let the punctuation tell you what to do. You'll want to carry a line right into the next line unless there is punctuation at the end of a line. You'll find the rhythm if you keep trying.

You will be writing your next literary analysis on *Emma*. This is due on Lesson 160. Be sure to budget your time appropriately. Here are your instructions.

- Novel Research Paper Requirements
    - Although you aren't going to begin writing right now, you will need to carefully review the requirements before you start. Here are the requirements:
        - Between 800 – 1100 words (2-3 pages)
        - Times New Roman or Arial font, 12 point, double spaced
        - MLA format (include correct page headings on all pages)
        - Must contain in-text citations, correctly formatted
        - Must contain at least five quotes/paraphrases: two from your novel and three from outside sources
        - Works Cited Page, correctly formatted
        - A minimum of five sources for your paper, including the novel. So you can count your novel as one source, and then find four more outside sources. You may have no more than three websites for your sources. Use books, journal articles, etc.

- Helpful hints for writing your paper
    - Take notes as you read your novel.
    - Write down important or interesting quotes with page numbers.
    - Write down interesting facts in your novel (setting, character actions, plot points, etc.)
    - Develop a potential thesis and look for information to support that as you read.
    - Look for outside sources as you read your novel. Keep a list of these (title, author, location, date, etc.)

- See the next page for your rubric for this assignment.

Lesson 153: *Emma* Literary Analysis Rubric Lit & Comp II LA

This is the grading rubric you will use for your literary analysis of *Emma*.

Content		
All information is factually correct 10	Most information is factually correct 9 - 4	Many factual errors/inconsistencies 3 - 1
Excellent background, context, and idea development 10	Adequate background, context, and idea development 9 - 4	Poor background, context, and idea development 3 - 1
Thesis is clear 10	Thesis is adequate 9 - 4	Thesis is poor 3 - 1
Excellent variety of sources 5	Adequate variety of sources 4 - 2	Inadequate variety of sources 1
Excellent discussion of detail 10	Adequate discussion of detail 9 - 4	Vague discussion of detail 3 - 1
Impressive depth of insight/analysis 10	Adequate depth of insight/analysis 9 - 4	Unexceptional insight/analysis 3 - 1
Effective conclusion/integration 10	Adequate conclusion/integration 9 – 4	Weak conclusion/integration 3 -1
Format and Style		
Excellent MLA style 5	Adequate MLA style 4-2	Poor MLA style 1
Clear organization 10	Adequate organization 9 - 4	Confusing organization 3 - 1
Smooth transitions 5	Adequate transitions 4 - 2	Awkward transitions 1
Correct grammar/no spelling mistakes 10	Few grammar errors/few spelling mistakes 9 - 4	Incorrect grammar/many spelling mistakes 3 - 1
Clean/legible manuscript 5	Adequate manuscript 4 – 2	Sloppy manuscript 1
Total Points:		(100 possible)

(Rubric adapted from GAVL, creative commons 3.0 [https://creativecommons.org/licenses/by/3.0/], cms.gavirtualschool.org/ Shared/ Language%20Arts/10thLitComp/01_NovelResearch/ResearchPaperGradingRubric.pdf)

Lesson 154: Malapropism Lit & Comp II LA

Read about malapropisms in your Reader, and then write a malapropism. Just one sentence is all it takes. Don't forget to work on your *Emma* literary analysis.

Lesson 155: *Much Ado About Nothing Writing* Lit & Comp II LA

- Can you describe any of the characters in the play? What have you learned about them? Write about it.
- Keep working on your literary analysis.

Lesson 156: *Much Ado About Nothing Writing* Lit & Comp II LA

- Can you find a line with word play in your Reader lesson? Copy it and cite it properly.
- Continue to work on your analysis.

Lesson 157: *Much Ado About Nothing Writing* Lit & Comp II LA

Write a diary entry for one of the characters.

Lesson 158: *Much Ado About Nothing* Writing   Lit & Comp II LA

Set a timer for 10 minutes. Write about one of the characters in the play. Write about the kind of person he is, the decision she makes, what's admirable or undesirable about the character. Is this someone you would want to be friends with? Why or why not? Record your score out of five according to the rubric in Lesson 49.

Lesson 159: *Much Ado About Nothing* Writing   Lit & Comp II LA

Here is a topic list for *Much Ado About Nothing* that you will use for several lessons. Today, choose a topic that makes sense at this point in the play. Set a timer and write. Using the rubric in Lesson 49, calculate your score and then **double it** and record out of 10.

1. Which love story do you feel is the play's main plot? Explain why you have chosen it and describe it completely. Then explain the role of the other love story.

2. Who are the leading characters of the play? (Choose two or three.) Explain why you think so. Who are the secondary characters and what point do they serve? How about the remaining characters?

3. Identify the scenes that use verse instead of prose. What effect does the use of verse have? Why is verse used in each place?

4. Write the play's prequel (the backstory or what happened before the time of the play) from a particular angle. For instance, what is the earlier relationship between Beatrice and Benedick? What is the family conflict and struggle between Don John and Don Pedro? What encounter did Claudio and Hero have before the play's beginning?

5. Write the play's sequel (the next chapter, what happens in the future) from a particular angle. What is in store for Don John? What punishments might Benedick have in mind for him? What is the future for Claudio and Hero? Beatrice and Benedick? Borachio and Margaret? Leonato?

6. What are the significant occurrences of a character taking special notice in the play? What examples of eavesdropping, observing, or otherwise noticing accomplished something important?

7. Why did Margaret participate in the window love scene with Borachio? What did he say to her before and after the scene? What did she tell Leonato about it when he questioned her? Write about these events from Margaret's perspective.

8. What changes would you make to the play if you rewrote it? Would you add/take out any events? Would you change the characters? Summarize your revised plot.

Lesson 160: *Much Ado About Nothing* Writing Lit & Comp II LA

This time, answer one of the questions raised in the class discussion notes (these are found in your Reader in Lesson 160). Answer in a complete paragraph. The first sentence should restate your question and let the reader know what you are answering. Include examples from the play. Record 5 points for a complete paragraph that restates the question and answers the question.

Your paper on *Emma* is due today. Score it according to the rubric found in Lesson 153.

Lesson 161: *Much Ado About Nothing* Writing Lit & Comp II LA

Answer another one of the questions raised in the class discussion notes (these are found in your Reader in Lesson 160). Answer in a complete paragraph. The first sentence should restate your question and let the reader know what you are answering. Include examples from the play. Record 5 points for a complete paragraph that restates the question and answers the question.

Lesson 162: *Much Ado About Nothing* Writing Lit & Comp II LA

Try your hand at writing a summary of the play. Give it to someone to read. Give yourself 5 points if they knew what the plot was when they were done reading.

Lesson 163: *Much Ado About Nothing* Quiz

Take this quiz on *Much Ado About Nothing*. Record your score out of 10 (potential for extra credit).

1. Who wants to marry Hero at the start of the play?

   a. Don John   b. Claudio   c. Benedick   d. Don Pedro

2. What happens to Hero when Don John sets her up?

   a. She goes insane.
   b. She marries Benedick.
   c. She runs away.
   d. She dies.

3. Which of these best describes Beatrice?

   a. She's naïve.
   b. She speaks her mind without worrying about etiquette.
   c. She is the play's biggest flirt.

4. Which character is the biggest flirt?

   a. Ursula   b. Margaret   c. Beatrice   d. Hero

5. Whom does Claudio agree to marry after splitting up with Hero?

   a. Beatrice
   b. Margaret
   c. Antonio's daughter
   d. Ursula

6. Whom does Antonio tell Leonato is in love with Hero?

   a. Benedick   b. Don Pedro   c. Don John   d. Claudio

7. What is Leonato?

   a. a war hero   b. a constable   c. a governor   d. a king

(continued on next page)

8. Who is the constable's constant companion?

    a. Verges　　　　　b. Balthasar　　　　　c. Conrade

9. How do Don John and Boracio decide to disrupt Hero and Claudio's marriage?

    a. By making Hero appear to be disrespectful of her family
    b. By making Claudio appear to be dead
    c. By making Hero appear to be cheating on Claudio

10. Who provides the most comic relief in the play?

    a. Conrade　　　　b. Don John　　　　c. Dogberry　　　　d. Leonato

11. Who works to bring Benedick and Beatrice back together?

    a. Claudio　　　　b. Don Pedro　　　　c. Boracio　　　　d. Conrade

12. Why is Beatrice so rude to Benedick?

    a. She doesn't trust men.　　　　c. He hurt her in the past.
    b. She is a snob.　　　　　　　　d. She doesn't want to marry.

13. Do Hero and Claudio eventually get married?

    a. yes　　　　　　　b. no

14. Who says, "A man loves the meat in his youth, that he cannot endure in his age"?

    a. Benedick　　　　b. Don John　　　　c. Don Pedro　　　　d. Claudio

15. Why does Don John dislike his brother, Don Pedro?

    a. He lost to Don Pedro in battle　　　　c. Don Pedro is the sole heir
    b. Don Pedro feels sorry for Don John　　d. all of these

- Complete the writing assignment on the next page.

Lesson 163: *Much Ado About Nothing Writing* Lit & Comp II LA

Choose a new topic from Lesson 159. Set a timer and write for 10 minutes. Using the rubric in Lesson 49, calculate your score and then **double it** and record out of 10.

Lesson 164: *Much Ado About Nothing Writing* Lit & Comp II LA

Choose TWO new topics on *Much Ado About Nothing* from Lesson 159. Set a timer and write for 20 minutes. Write BY HAND for SAT practice. The SAT requires a handwritten essay done in 25 minutes. Using the rubric in Lesson 49, calculate your score for each and **double the score for each.**

Lesson 165: Editing

Read about editing and proofreading. Make sure you understand the best ways to go about the process and what to look for.

Editing

- Editing happens after you finish your first draft. You'll reread what you've written and make sure your paper flows, is well-organized, transitions smoothly, etc. Here are some areas to check:
  - Content
    - Verify that you've done everything required by the assignment. You also want to make sure you don't have information included that doesn't really pertain to what you're writing about.

  - Structure
    - Make sure your paper has an introduction and a conclusion. Your thesis should be clear and included in your introduction. Every paragraph should be related to your thesis and flow in a logical order with clear transitions.

  - Clarity
    - Is your paper clear? Do you need to define any terms? A way to check for clarity is to read your paper line by line backwards. That way you can see if each sentence makes sense on its own.

  - Style
    - Check to make sure your tone is appropriate to the assignment. A research paper shouldn't sound like you're conversing with a friend. Ensure you haven't repeated words unnecessarily.

  - Citations
    - Verify that you have followed the proper format for citing your sources, including any quotes or paraphrases you've used in your paper.

Proofreading

- Proofreading is the last step of the editing process, and it focuses on spelling, punctuation, and grammar mistakes. There's no reason to proofread until you've made all of your other edits.
  - Spell checkers and grammar checkers are limited, but can be helpful. Feel free to use them, but be sure to actually check these things for yourself as well.

  - The best way to catch everything is to proofread for one thing at a time – do a pass focused on spelling, then one focused on punctuation, etc.

- o Reading out loud can help you catch things you might not otherwise catch. You'll also want to read slowly so your brain doesn't fill in missing words or gloss over errors.
    - ▪ Check for organization, transitions, unnecessary repetition, and obviously grammar, spelling, and punctuation mistakes.

- **Tips for effective editing and proofreading**
    - o Don't attempt to edit or proofread as soon as you're done writing. Give yourself some time away from your work so it's not as familiar. This involves advanced planning! If you can set it aside for a day or two, that's great. If all you have is 20 minutes, let that be enough. Approaching your writing with fresh eyes will help you catch everything you need to catch during the editing process.

    - o Having a list of what to look for will also help guide your proofreading time. Your rubric or a general editing checklist will be helpful.

    - o Try different ways of proofreading. Some people work well reading straight off the computer screen. Others find it's easier to print the paper out and use a pen.

    - o Work in a quiet place! Editing or proofreading in front of the TV, while working out, or trying to socialize with a friend will definitely make it difficult to catch everything.

    - o Don't try to do it all at once. When you feel your brain drifting, take a break.

    - o Go slowly. Writing mistakes are often the result of rushing. Especially if you haven't had a break from your writing, your brain can read what you know you meant to write instead of what you actually wrote. Give your eyes time to spot the errors.

    - o Reading aloud can help you notice omitted words, run-on sentences, organizational issues, missing transitions, etc.

    - o Look for common mistakes we've tried to combat throughout this course. There is a list of commonly mixed up words in Lesson 1. We've gone over the fact that not all words that end in s need an apostrophe. Remember about subject/verb agreement and parallelism. Looking for errors in all of these common areas will help you find problem spots.

    - o Check for other common errors. Sentence fragments, dangling modifiers, unclear pronouns, and omitted or extra commas are all things that are common errors that we've learned about over the years through Easy Peasy Language Arts.

Lesson 165: Nonfiction Literary Terms

Read the nonfiction literary terms. Go over any you're unfamiliar with. Review Lesson 95 about the different types of nonfiction.

Allusion: a brief reference to a person, place, thing, event, or idea in history or literature. Allusions conjure up biblical authority, scenes from Shakespeare's plays, historic figures, wars, etc.

Anecdote: a short account of an incident or event of an interesting or amusing nature. It's a brief story to entertain or make a point.

Archetype: universal symbols that evoke deep and sometimes unconscious response in a reader. In literature, characters, images, and themes that symbolically embody universal meanings and basic human experiences – regardless of when or where they live – are considered archetypes.

Autobiography: a story of a person's life written by that person. It is nonfiction.

Bibliography: a list of source materials used or consulted in the preparation of a work or that are referred to in the text.

Caricature: a picture or description greatly exaggerating the peculiarities or defects of a person or thing.

Chronicle: a chronological record of events; a history.

Cliché: an idea or expression that has become tired and trite from overuse, its freshness and clarity having worn off. They are usually a sign of weak writing.

Coherence: logical interconnection.

Connotation: the associated or secondary meaning of a word or expression in addition to its primary or literal meaning.

Denotation: the explicit (dictionary) or direct meanings of a word or expression; it does NOT include the ideas or meanings suggested by it.

Dialect: a type of informal diction (word choice). Dialects are spoken by definable groups of people from a particular geographic region, economic group, or social class.

Diction: a writer's choice of words, phrases, sentence structures, and figurative language which combine to help create meaning.

Didactic: intended to teach a lesson.

Editorial: an article in a newspaper or other periodical or broadcast statement presenting the opinion of the publishers or editors or of station owners or station managers.

Elaboration: the act of developing or expanding in great detail.

Essay: a short nonfiction work that deals with one subject. The author might give an opinion, try to persuade or simply narrate an interesting event. Essays may be formal or informal. Formal essays examine a topic in a thorough, serious, and highly organized manner. Informal essays reflect the writer's feelings and personality.

Eulogy: a formal speech of praise, usually for someone who is dead.

Euphemism: a word or phrase used in place of a more direct but distasteful or offensive word or phrase.

Narrator: the teller of a story or other narrative. A narrator may be the author speaking in his or her own voice or a character or persona created by the author to tell the story. A narrator may stand inside the story, telling events from a first-person point of view, or outside the story, telling the events from the third-person point of view.

Intrusive narrator: a storyteller who keeps interrupting the narrative to address the reader directly to make extended personal comments about the characters or about other matters.

Unreliable narrator: Characters telling their stories in first person are often unreliable because they have attitudes or emotions that distort the story they tell.

Oration: a formal speech.

Paradox: a statement that, while apparently self-contradictory, is essentially true. Example: Success is counted sweetest by those who never succeed.

Parallelism: the technique of showing that words, phrases, clauses, or larger structures are comparable in content and importance by placing them side by side and making them similar in form.

Paraphrase: a restatement of an expression or a passage that retains the meaning of the original but presents it in different words and often in a different form; a rewording.

Periodical: published with a fixed time between a series of articles (i.e., magazines).

Plagiarism: Using another writer's ideas or words as one's own. Plagiarism ranges from deliberate literary theft to inept paraphrasing to unconscious borrowing.

Prose: all forms of ordinary writing and speech lacking the sustained and regular rhythmic patterns of poetry. Prose is characterized by the sort of plain, straightforward statement found in everyday speech written in paragraph form. It is the language of essays, short stories, and novels.

Requiem: a chant, dirge, or poem for the dead; from the Roman Catholic mass for the dead.

Rhetorical question: a question asked that is not intended to be answered.

Sarcasm: Harsh, cutting, personal remarks to or about someone, not necessarily ironic.

Satire: any form of literature that blends ironic humor and wit with criticism for the purpose of ridiculing folly, vice, stupidity, etc. in individuals and institutions. Satire differs from comedy in that it seeks to correct, improve, or reform through ridicule, while comedy aims simply to amuse. It differs from a mere insult in the sharp wit of its presentation.

Fact: something that can be proven true by concrete information.

Opinion: the belief of a person. It can't be proven.

Sensory Details: information you can observe through any of your senses.

Statistics: a fact based on numbers.

Comparing and Contrasting: "compare" shows how things are similar (alike); "contrast" shows how things are different.

Cause and Effect: one event causes a second event to occur.

Explaining a process: you tell how something works or how to do something.

Editorial (Political) Cartoon: a cartoon that expresses the issues of the day.

Captions: the words spoken by the artist or characters in the cartoon.

Symbol: something that stands for or represents something else.

Humor: comical.

Stereotype: eliminates anything unique about an individual by exaggerating features associated with a group.

Irony: portrays differences between what is said and what is meant (verbal), between what is seen and what is real (dramatic), and between what is expected and what actually happens (situational)

Bias: a prejudiced outlook; a personal or distorted view.

Propaganda: the spreading of ideas, information, or rumor to either help or injure a person.

Lesson 166: Journal Prompt

Set your timer and write for ten minutes. Choose another prompt from Lesson 49's list and score it according to the rubric.

Fill out this fable chart for "The Story of the Little Red Hen."

Title and Author				
Animal Characters				
Human Characteristics				
Setting				
Situation				
Conflict or Problem				
Climax				
Falling Action				
Resolution				
Moral or Lesson				

- Read about your next writing assignment on the next page.

Lesson 169: Fable Writing Assignment

Read about your next writing assignment. Get started on it. It is due on Lesson 172. Make a list of what needs to get done and make a schedule for when you should complete each part. On Lesson 172 you should be rereading the rubric and making final edits.

- Write an essay with a thesis based on the main idea of one of the fables you've read in this unit. Your paper should follow the basic essay structure: state the thesis in the introduction, followed by examples in the body of the essay that support the thesis, and then a conclusion that ties it all together.
  - You will be using one or more of the fables you've read as the basis of the thesis for your essay. You are allowed to refer directly to the fable in your paper, but you are not required to do so.

- Your thesis should be in your own words. If you use a direct quotation from one of the fables, be sure to put it in quotation marks and cite it. Your thesis should not just be a restatement of a moral from the fable, but rather it should show how the idea from the fable relates to your paper.

- The body of your paper should contain specific examples that support your thesis. This will be a more narrative-style essay, showcasing personal anecdotes or experiences that support your thesis.

- Here is the rubric for your fable essay. It will be worth 100 points:

  1. 10 points for Moral/Lesson from fable identified
  2. 15 points for Thesis Statement
  3. 30 points for Supporting points/body paragraphs
  4. 15 points for Adequate conclusion
  5. 15 points for MLA formatting
  6. 15 points for Personal connections

  Total Points: 100

Lesson 170: Fable Chart

Fill out this fable chart for "The Ugly Duckling."

Title and Author				
Animal Characters				
Human Characteristics				
Setting				
Situation				
Conflict or Problem				
Climax				
Falling Action				
Resolution				
Moral or Lesson				

- You may want to consider taking the Analyzing and Interpreting Literature CLEP test after this course. If you pass, you would get college credit. You could also label this as an honors course. Even if you aren't going to take the test, it won't hurt you to try a practice question each day. Please access the online course for links to the practice questions if you're interested.

Finish your fable assignment. Score it according to the rubric in Lesson 169. Record your score. Now read over your final assignment. You can choose any topic. It will be due on Lesson 179.

Non-Fiction Writing Assignment

- For this project, you will delve into the realm of nonfiction and find interesting facts about a particular event in history. You will create a newsletter detailing points about the event, then you will write a 30 – 60 second audio podcast that summarizes the event.

Step 1 – Newsletter
- For this part of the project, you will create a newsletter that highlights details of the chosen event. It should contain at least 5 sections, with varying information from the time period (people, places, occurrences, social information, and entertainment). It may also contain more, such as weather, horoscopes, etc. Each section is expected to have at least two to three well-developed paragraphs, with solid information. It will also need to include at least three graphics, but may contain more.

Guidelines for sections:
- **People** – 2-3 people who were important during this time period/event; why they were important; how they influenced the region, world, etc. (If it was a Civil War newsletter, it might discuss Abraham Lincoln, General Sherman, and Robert E. Lee.)

- **Places** – where the event(s) took place, time of the event, etc. (The Civil War newsletter might cover areas from Charleston through Atlanta.)

- **Occurrences** – specifics of event(s) of that period. (The Civil War newsletter might cover the burning of Atlanta or Battle of Gettysburg.)

- **Social Information** – what was going on in the community at that time. (The Civil War newsletter might cover how slavery impacted the war.)

- **Entertainment** – how people spent their time during this event. (The Civil War newsletter might cover the dances of the time period, war effort events, etc.)

Step 2 – Podcast
- Write a podcast for the event summarizing it. You can do this live for an audience or record yourself. It should be less than a minute.

- You will need to include a works cited page (MLA format) in addition to your newsletter and audio recording. This can be on a separate page and should include all works used to gather your information, as well as the images you use.

Lesson 172: Non-Fiction Writing Rubric

Here is your rubric for your nonfiction writing assignment.

Category	4 points	3 points	2 points	1 point
Originality	Shows a large amount of original thought. Ideas are creative and inventive.	Shows some original thought. Work shows new ideas and insights.	Uses other people's ideas (giving them credit), but there is little evidence of original thinking.	Uses other people's ideas, but does not give them credit.
Requirements	All requirements are met and exceeded.	All requirements are met.	One requirement was not completely met.	More than one requirement was not completely met.
Attractiveness	Makes excellent use of font, color, graphics, effects, etc. to enhance the presentation.	Makes good use of font, color, graphics, effects, etc. to enhance the presentation.	Makes use of font, color, graphics, effects, etc. but occasionally these detract from the presentation content.	Use of font, color, graphics, effects, etc. but these often distract from the presentation content.
Content	Subject knowledge is excellent.	Includes essential knowledge about the topic. Subject knowledge appears to be good.	Includes essential information about the topic but there are factual errors.	Content is minimal OR there are several factual errors.
Mechanics	No misspellings or grammatical errors.	Three or fewer misspellings and/or mechanical errors.	Four misspellings and/or grammatical errors.	More than four errors in spelling or grammar.

You should be studying for your final exam. Study your vocabulary words. Look over your tests and the questions that you missed. Study any words you've had trouble with this year. Review the various literary terms presented in this book. Set a timer and study for a set amount of time each day leading up to your final exam. You will also want to be able to answer these summary questions about your various units:

Novel Research[4]
- What can I learn from a novel?
- Why are good research skills important?
- What is the theme of your novel?

Poetry Unit One[5]
- What are some of the intentions or uses of poetry?
- How effective are poems in expressing the thoughts of writers?
- How could you use poetry in your life?

Short Story[6]
1. What can you predict or infer about a story by its title?
2. Where do you see short story elements in your life?

Nonfiction Unit One[7]
- What can you learn from nonfiction writing?
- What are some critical historical events about which you wish to learn more information?
- Why is nonfiction writing important?

Arthurian Legends[8]
- Do you believe that chivalry still exists today?
- Stories of heroic deeds have been told for centuries. Where can you see heroism today?

Poetry Unit Two[9]
- What in your life could be expressed as a poem?
- What is the goal of poetry or descriptive writing?

---

[4] (Questions from GAVL, creative commons 3.0 [https://creativecommons.org/licenses/by/3.0/], http://cms.gavirtualschool.org/Shared/Language%20Arts/10thLitComp/01_NovelResearch/index.html)

[5] (Questions from GAVL, creative commons 3.0 [https://creativecommons.org/licenses/by/3.0/], http://cms.gavirtualschool.org/Shared/Language%20Arts/10thLitComp/02_PoetryOne/index.html)

[6] (Questions from GAVL, creative commons 3.0 [https://creativecommons.org/licenses/by/3.0/], http://cms.gavirtualschool.org/Shared/Language%20Arts/10thLitComp/03_ShortStoriesOne/index.html)

[7] (Questions from GAVL, creative commons 3.0 [https://creativecommons.org/licenses/by/3.0/], http://cms.gavirtualschool.org/Shared/Language%20Arts/10thLitComp/05_NonfictionOne/index.html)

[8] (Questions from GAVL, creative commons 3.0 [https://creativecommons.org/licenses/by/3.0/], http://cms.gavirtualschool.org/Shared/Language%20Arts/10thLitComp/06_TheArthurianLegends/index.html)

[9] (Questions from GAVL, creative commons 3.0 [https://creativecommons.org/licenses/by/3.0/], http://cms.gavirtualschool.org/Shared/Language%20Arts/10thLitComp/09_PoetryTwo/index.html)

Shakespeare Much Ado[10]
- How do the topics of Shakespeare's works connect to today?
- Are trickery and deceit okay if the end result is good?
- Does love conquer all?

Traditions[11]
- How do you judge the usefulness of advice?
- From where do you draw wisdom?
- What are the purposes of fables, proverbs, sayings, etc.?

Nonfiction Unit Two[12]
- Why might someone write a biography or an autobiography?
- What events in your life might you want to share with generations later?
- What is the purpose of nonfiction writing?

Lesson 179: Non-Fiction Writing Assignment   Lit & Comp II LA

Grade your non-fiction writing assignment according to the rubric in Lesson 172. Record your score on your grade sheet.

---

[10] (Questions from GAVL, creative commons 3.0 [https://creativecommons.org/licenses/by/3.0/], http://cms.gavirtualschool.org/Shared/Language%20Arts/10thLitComp/10_ShakespeareMuchAdo/index.html)

[11] (Questions from GAVL, creative commons 3.0 [https://creativecommons.org/licenses/by/3.0/], http://cms.gavirtualschool.org/Shared/Language%20Arts/10thLitComp/11_Traditions/index.html)

[12] (Questions from GAVL, creative commons 3.0 [https://creativecommons.org/licenses/by/3.0/], http://cms.gavirtualschool.org/Shared/Language%20Arts/10thLitComp/12_NonfictionTwo/index.html)

Take your final exam. It is worth 100 points: 50 vocabulary questions each worth 1 point, 25 multiple choice questions each worth 1 point, and 5 essay questions each worth 5 points. Record your score on your grade sheet.

Vocabulary: circle the answer that *best* fits.

1. The _____ of animal noises gave me a headache.
    a. cacophony   b. longevity   c. demeanor   d. veracity

2. His _____ behavior earned him the respect of the squad.
    a. fraudulent   b. insidious   c. exemplary   d. sacrosanct

3. Sometimes quiet people become quite _____ when they're nervous.
    a. nautical   b. loquacious   c. abstract   d. translucent

4. A synonym for *shy*.
    a. docile   b. rebuke   c. demure   d. integrity

5. The _____ between a boy and his dog is unparalleled.
    a. congregation   b. fuse   c. orator   d. camaraderie

6. Our _____ lives have made us forget how to appreciate art.
    a. prosaic   b. recalcitrant   c. intransigent   d. lucrative

7. Don't _____ your sister; get along!
    a. anticipate   b. antagonize   c. depict   d. transmute

8. The clerk wouldn't cash the _____ check.
    a. impassive   b. pertinacious   c. recalcitrant   d. fraudulent

9. A synonym for *annoy*.
    a. transmute   b. vex   c. anticipate   d. oppose

10. An antonym of *concrete*.
    a. abstract   b. impassive   c. submissive   d. propitious

11. The _____ teenager gets into trouble often.
    a. lucrative   b. nautical   c. recalcitrant   d. impassive

12. The politician created an ad to _____ his opponent.
    a. generalize   b. vilify   c. expiate   d. generalize

13. The juror had the _____ to challenge the expert's opinion.
    a. effrontery   b. prosperity   c. constituent   d. connotation

14. You should not _____ your own worth.
    a. expiate   b. deprecate   c. generalize   d. expunge

15. The girl gave a _____ shrug.
    a. trilateral   b. sanctimonious   c. vicarious   d. nonchalant

16. The fur coat was a bit _____ for the funeral.
    a. intuitive   b. consecutive   c. ostentatious   d. trenchant

17. Will the Florida _____ be joining the assembly?
    a. grandeur   b. invective   c. contingent   d. surfeit

18. The _____ display got us all in the Christmas spirit.
    a. jubilant   b. clairvoyant   c. redundant   d. circuitous

19. The aspirin served to _____ his pain.
    a. impute   b. palliate   c. surfeit   d. reflect

20. The drama queen behaved in a _____ way toward even the smallest incident.
    a. prudent   b. incompatible   c. maudlin   d. inchoate

21. The newspaper's _____ of the rally infuriated its organizers.
    a. invective   b. contingent   c. grandiloquence   d. panacea

22. The scientist had a _____ approach to dealing with the water shortage.
    a. pragmatic   b. prurient   c. facetious   d. correlate

23. The _____ inquiry about my health was appreciated.
   a. unilateral   b. skeptical   c. solicitous   d. incongruous

24. The _____ of business owners sponsored a scholarship.
   a. differential   b. coalition   c. jurisdiction   d. sycophant

25. Playing in the basketball game left me _____.
   a. parched   b. precipitous   c. relevant   d. incongruous

26. The _____ mess of a room took hours to clean.
   a. pugnacious   b. incontrovertible   c. sustainable   d. jumbled

27. We were _____ to the trail of ants coming in overnight.
   a. uninspired   b. oblivious   c. haughty   d. obsequious

28. The _____ didn't gel as much as the chemist had anticipated.
   a. solution   b. compassion   c. criterion   d. pariah

29. Splitting all the candy was the most _____ thing I could think of.
   a. fastidious   b. fallacious   c. indefatigable   d. equitable

30. The toddler didn't want to _____ his sister's toy.
   a. preclude   b. collaborate   c. relinquish   d. justify

31. With _____ studying, he received a great score on the SAT.
   a. solipsistic   b. taciturn   c. diligent   d. uninspired

32. The desire to belong is a _____ one.
   a. qualitative   b. primeval   c. tedious   d. pretentious

33. The _____ box was hard to get through the door.
   a. tactile   b. latent   c. cumbersome   d. resilient

34. As _____ as it sounds, I prefer dining at country clubs.
   a. pretentious   b. obsolete   c. quantitative   d. anachronistic

35. The _____ clothing ruined the movie for me.
    a. anachronistic   b. wistful   c. tantamount   d. benevolent

36. My sister tried to _____ sickness to get out of doing chores.
    a. rescind   b. feign   c. complement   d. discredit

37. A synonym for *smelly*.
    a. multifarious   b. vacuous   c. officious   d. fetid

38. The baby held my finger in his _____ little fist.
    a. tenacious   b. odious   c. ingenuous   d. strenuous

39. If you _____ too much you'll miss out on our weekend plans.
    a. exacerbate   b. procrastinate   c. disseminate   d. decry

40. The _____ task of raking the leaves was somehow soothing to me.
    a. mundane   b. hypothetical   c. concurrent   d. wizened

41. Their _____ expressions told me it was time to end the lecture.
    a. multifarious   b. officious   c. vacuous   d. strenuous

42. The _____ snowstorms kept us home for weeks.
    a. perfunctory   b. perpetual   c. ribald   d. opportune

43. My _____ rug adds life to the room.
    a. rancorous   b. perfunctory   c. variegated   d. stringent

44. The athlete lifted weights to _____ his body.
    a. condition   b. omit   c. demean   d. promulgate

45. You need to _____ the chicken in the broth to keep it from drying out.
    a. submerge   b. ribald   c. demagogue   d. zephyr

46. His teenager answered most questions with _____ nods.
    a. omnipotent   b. anonymous   c. perfunctory   d. florid

47.   The _____ tip helped the police find the missing car.
       a. conditional   b. inimical   c. anonymous   d. prolific

48.   A series of _____ circumstances helped advance his political career.
       a. fortuitous   b. rancorous   c. omnipotent   d. limpid

49.   A terrible and _____ argument erupted.
       a. conditional   b. variegated   c. tractable   d. rancorous

50.   Alyssa rushed out of the room in an apparent _____.
       a. demagogue   b. dither   c. burnish   d. zest

Literary Terms: Circle the best choice.

1. The reoccurrence of the same words, lines, or stanzas to enhance the mood:

       a. repetition   b. symbol   c. rhyme   d. hyperbole

2. The protagonist is the character who opposes the main character.
       a. true   b. false

3. The repetition of initial sounds in neighboring words:
       a. hyperbole   b. rhyme   c. alliteration   d. repetition

4. The main idea in a literary work which unifies the plot, characters, setting, and other elements of the story:
       a. setting   b. theme   c. plot   d. character

5. When something concrete stands for something that is abstract:
       a. repetition   b. symbol   c. hyperbole   d. stanza

6. A speech made by one character that other characters do not hear at the time:
       a. dialogue   b. monologue   c. soliloquy   d. aside

7. A difference between what is meant or expected and what actually happens:
       a. irony   b. foreshadowing   c. hyperbole   d. point of view

8. A conversation between two or more characters:
   a. dialogue   b. aside   c. monologue   d. soliloquy

9. A speech made by one character alone on stage to show his or her feelings:
   a. aside   b. dialogue   c. soliloquy   d. monologue

10. The antagonist is the main character, often the hero or heroine of the story.
   a. true   b. false

11. A struggle presented within a story between two opposing forces:
   a. conflict   b. plot   c. setting   d. motif

12. The point of highest intensity in a story:
   a. suspense   b. conflict   c. climax   d. plot

13. A direct comparison between two unlike things, not using "like" or "as":
   a. metaphor   b. stanza   c. simile   d. repetition

14. The time, place, and environment of a story.
   a. theme   b. plot   c. character   d. setting

15. The feeling of uncertainty about what is going to happen next.
   a. suspense   b. character   c. theme   d. foreshadowing

16. A work of literature meant to be performed:
   a. plot   b. drama   c. novel   d. tragedy

17. An extreme exaggeration, used to make a point:
   a. alliteration   b. simile   c. symbol   d. hyperbole

18. A drama in which the main character experiences extreme sorrow:
   a. conflict   b. tragedy   c. drama   d. comedy

19. The voice in which the story is told:
   a. prose   b. point of view   c. conflict   d. novel

20. Clues or details about what will happen later in the story:
    a. plot   b. suspense   c. foreshadowing   d. setting

21. A comparison between two unlike thing, using "like" or "as":
    a. symbol   b. simile   c. metaphor   d. alliteration

22. A long speech made by one character:
    a. aside   b. point of view   c. dialogue   d. monologue

23. A reference to another person, place, event, or literary work/character:
    a. simile   b. metaphor   c. hyperbole   d. allusion

24. A group of lines in a poem, like paragraphs in an essay:
    a. stanza   b. metaphor   c. rhyme   d. simile

25. Repetition of the same ending sounds in words:
    a. rhyme   b. alliteration   c. repetition   d. metaphor

Essay Questions: answers must be in a complete paragraph. Each paragraph will be scored as follows: 1 point: thesis statement, 1 point: conclusion, 3 points: details/examples

Answer both of the following two questions.
- What is the goal of poetry or descriptive writing?
- Why is nonfiction writing important?

Answer any three of the following questions.
- Do you believe that chivalry still exists today?
- Stories of heroic deeds have been told for centuries. Where can you see heroism today?
- Does love conquer all?
- How do you judge the usefulness of advice?
- From where do you draw wisdom?
- Why might someone write a biography or an autobiography?
- What events in your life might you want to share with generations later?

Be sure to grade your final exam and add your score to your grade sheet. Your final task for the year is to figure out your course grade!

- First add up your scores for this quarter and write that number down.
- Add up the total possible points and write that number down.
- Divide those numbers. Your total earned divided by total possible. Move the decimal point over two places to the right for your percentage grade for the fourth quarter.
- Now add your four quarter scores together. Add your four quarter points possible together. Divide your total scores earned by total points possible across the entire course.
- This is your percent grade for the entire course. Next to that you can write your letter grade. 90-100 is an A, 80-89 is a B, 70-79 is a C.
- Congratulations on finishing Literature and Composition II!

Answers

Lesson 3: Plagiarism Quiz

1. Plagiarism can be avoided by thoroughly citing sources.

True

2. Ideas cannot really be stolen.

False

3. You can use a Works Cited list for listing the sources you've used.

True

4. If you paraphrase or summarize a document, you don't have to cite the source.

False

5. Sometimes something popular, like playing covers of copyrighted songs, can still be considered plagiarism.

True

Lesson 4: Evaluating Sources

1. To check authority of a website, you should look for the author/sponsor and contact information.

True

2. All websites can be trusted as sources.

False

3. Some of the most reliable website extensions include .com and .net.

False

4. Bias is not important when evaluating the credibility of a website.

False

5. If the author of the article cites sources, it's more likely to be accurate.

True

Lesson 5: Literary Terms Quiz

Take this literary terms quiz and record your score on your grade sheet. This should be review.

1. Which term refers to the struggle in the story, usually between the protagonist and antagonist?

a. setting   b. theme   **(c.) conflict**

2. The protagonist is _____ .

(a) the main/central character, sometimes called the hero
b. the character who opposes the main character, typically creating the conflict
c. the voice used to tell the story

3. The time and location in which the story takes place is the _____ .

a. point of view   **(b) setting**   c. theme

4. The antagonist is _____ .

a. the main/central character, sometimes called the hero
(b) the character who opposes the main character, typically creating the conflict
c. the voice used to tell the story

5. The theme of a novel is _____ .

a. the struggle between characters
(b) the main idea; the point of the story
c. the time and place in which the story takes place

Lesson 8: Sentence Quiz

Identify whether each group of words is a run-on, complete sentence, or fragment. Check your answers and learn from any mistakes.

1. Which was created in 1979.
   a. run-on   b. complete sentence   **(c) fragment**

2. She needed the ingredients for cookies, she went to the store.
   (a) run-on   b. complete sentence   c. fragment

3. Needed the materials for the science project.
   a. run-on   b. complete sentence   **(c) fragment**

4. Lee Giles created Easy Peasy curriculum and Genesis Curriculum.
   a. run-on   **(b) complete sentence**   c. fragment

5. We have too much homework, we have no time for fun.
   (a) run-on   b. complete sentence   c. fragment

6. When we have to stay up too late.
   a. run-on   b. complete sentence   **(c) fragment**

7. The dog chewed up the shoes, he made a huge mess.
   (a) run-on   b. complete sentence   c. fragment

8. Reading is a great way to pass the time.
   a. run-on   **(b) complete sentence**   c. fragment

9. After I spilled taco seasoning everywhere.
   a. run-on   b. complete sentence   **(c) fragment**

10. Compared to all the other bakers, she makes the best cake.
    a. run-on   **(b) complete sentence**   c. fragment

Lesson 9: Poetic Devices Crossword

Complete the crossword puzzle.

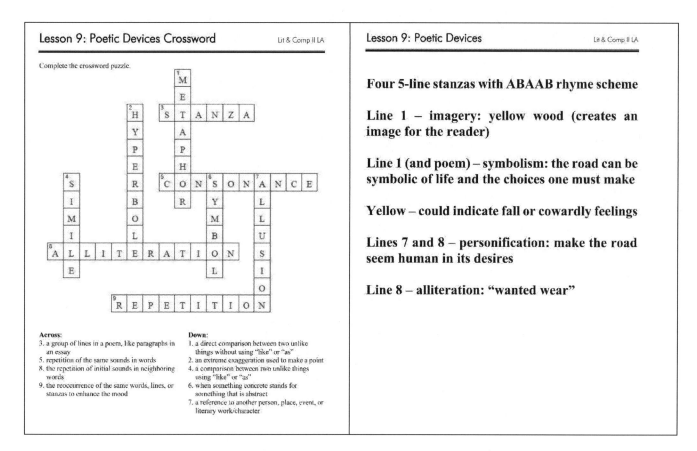

Across:
3. a group of lines in a poem, like paragraphs in an essay
5. repetition of the same sounds in words
8. the repetition of initial sounds in neighboring words
9. the reoccurrence of the same words, lines, or stanzas to enhance the mood

Down:
1. a direct comparison between two unlike things without using "like" or "as"
2. an extreme exaggeration used to make a point
4. a comparison between two unlike things using "like" or "as"
6. when something concrete stands for something that is abstract
7. a reference to another person, place, event, or literary work/character

---

Lesson 9: Poetic Devices

Four 5-line stanzas with ABAAB rhyme scheme

Line 1 – imagery: yellow wood (creates an image for the reader)

Line 1 (and poem) – symbolism: the road can be symbolic of life and the choices one must make

Yellow – could indicate fall or cowardly feelings

Lines 7 and 8 – personification: make the road seem human in its desires

Line 8 – alliteration: "wanted wear"

Lesson 10: Analyzing Poetry

Which line is an example of simile?
a. "And I will come again, my luve"
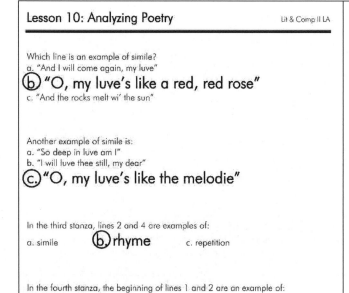
b "O, my luve's like a red, red rose"
c. "And the rocks melt wi' the sun"

Another example of simile is:
a. "So deep in luve am I"
b. "I will luve thee still, my dear"
c "O, my luve's like the melodie"

In the third stanza, lines 2 and 4 are examples of:
a. simile   **b rhyme**   c. repetition

In the fourth stanza, the beginning of lines 1 and 2 are an example of:
a repetition   b. hyperbole   c. simile

Lesson 12: Sentence Quiz

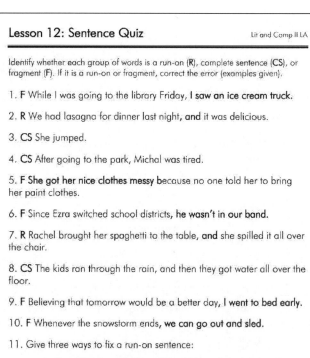

Identify whether each group of words is a run-on (R), complete sentence (CS), or fragment (F). If it is a run-on or fragment, correct the error (examples given).

1. F While I was going to the library Friday, **I saw an ice cream truck.**

2. R We had lasagna for dinner last night**, and** it was delicious.

3. CS She jumped.

4. CS After going to the park, Michal was tired.

5. F She got her nice clothes messy because no one told her to bring her paint clothes.

6. F Since Ezra switched school districts, **he wasn't in our band.**

7. R Rachel brought her spaghetti to the table**, and** she spilled it all over the chair.

8. CS The kids ran through the rain, and then they got water all over the floor.

9. F Believing that tomorrow would be a better day, **I went to bed early.**

10. F Whenever the snowstorm ends, **we can go out and sled.**

11. Give three ways to fix a run-on sentence:

Many choices: Add a semicolon, add a period, add a comma with a conjunction, add a subordinating conjunction, add an em dash

Lesson 12: Sentence Quiz

What choice best describes the group of words presented?

1. I like apples, she likes bananas, he likes oranges.
   (a.) run-on   b. complete sentence   c. fragment

2. With all this rain, my yard is going to flood soon.
   a. run-on   **(b.) complete sentence**   c. fragment

3. I went to the movies, I went to the store.
   (a.) run-on   b. complete sentence   c. fragment

4. After the biggest earthquake I've ever experienced in my life.
   a. run-on   b. complete sentence   **(c.) fragment**

5. We should go to the store because we are out of bread.
   a. run-on   **(b.) complete sentence**   c. fragment

6. My dog ran away, but then he came back.
   a. run-on   **(b.) complete sentence**   c. fragment

7. When you write with a pen with blue ink and it smudges.
   a. run-on   b. complete sentence   **(c.) fragment**

8. We exercised all week, we prepared for the track meet.
   (a.) run-on   b. complete sentence   c. fragment

9. The winter catalogue had a sale on sweaters, boots, and scarves.
   a. run-on   **(b.) complete sentence**   c. fragment

10. All my dirty laundry.
    a. run-on   b. complete sentence   **(c.) fragment**

Lesson 13: Poetic Devices

Choose which poetic/literary device is represented in each example.

1. She sells sea shells by the seashore.
   a. consonance   b. assonance   **(c.) alliteration**   d. oxymoron

2. The BOOM of the fireworks shook the windows.
   a. simile   **(b.) onomatopoeia**   c. metaphor   d. personification

3. My mom tells me to clean by room a thousand times a day.
   (a.) hyperbole   b. allusion   c. simile   d. metaphor

4. The tree was a fortress, protecting our picnic from the rain.
   a. consonance   **(b.) metaphor**   c. alliteration   d. simile

5. The black cat attacked the wrapping paper.
   a. allusion   **(b.) assonance**   c. alliteration   d. repetition

6. The clouds were like fluffy cotton candy.
   a. metaphor   b. onomatopoeia   c. oxymoron   **(d.) simile**

7. He lifted the couch with Herculean strength.
   (a.) allusion   b. consonance   c. cliché   d. metaphor

8. The wind whispered through the leaves.
   a. hyperbole   b. assonance   **(c.) personification**   d. repetition

9. We must, we MUST get there in time!
   (a.) repetition   b. hyperbole   c. metaphor   d. simile

10. It's the same difference.
    a. onomatopoeia   b. alliteration   **(c.) oxymoron**   d. allusion

Lesson 20: Passive Voice

Rewrite the following sentences to change the voice from passive to active. NOTE: not all of the sentences are in passive voice. Pay attention!

Flight of Her Life was written by Jennifer Appel.

Jennifer Appel wrote *Flight of Her Life*.

I was amazed by the weatherman's lack of accuracy.

The weatherman's lack of accuracy amazed me.

A surprise thunderstorm soaked us as we finished up our hike.

(This sentence is already in the active voice.)

Late last night, I was told the shocking news by my son.

Late last night, my son told me the shocking news.

With three weeks to go in the semester, we were informed of a huge new assignment by our professor.

With three weeks to go in the semester, our professor informed us of a huge new assignment.

The hockey puck was fired off the glass by the defenseman.

The defenseman fired the hockey puck off the glass.

Lesson 21: Active and Passive Voice

Determine whether each sentence is in the active or the passive voice.

1. The two girls sometimes draw pictures.
   (active)   passive

2. The stereos are made in China.
   active   **(passive)**

3. Many trees were damaged by the hurricane.
   active   **(passive)**

4. Mr. Dossett conducted the band.
   (active)   passive

5. Bryce was riding his bike.
   (active)   passive

6. The Olympian ran the 100-yard dash.
   (active)   passive

7. Walls have been demolished.
   active   **(passive)**

8. The Dead Sea Scrolls are written in Hebrew.
   active   **(passive)**

9. You should have come with us.
   (active)   passive

10. The clothes were bought on sale.
    active   **(passive)**

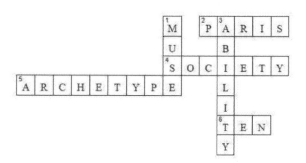

Across:
2. Took Helen back to Troy to marry her
4. An epic hero must possess traits that are important to _____
5. A character that occurs in some stories across all cultures
6. The Trojan War lasted for _____ years.

Down:
1. A goddess who helps the main character in an epic poem
3. One of the characteristics of an epic poem is having a hero who has superhuman _____.

Book I
1. Where is Odysseus in this book?

Odysseus is imprisoned on an island by the daughter of Atlas, Calypso, who wants Odysseus for herself.

2. How is Athena disguised?

Athena is disguised as a stranger, Mentes, the Taphian leader.

3. Why do Penelope and Telemachus need Odysseus?

Suitors have come and are eating enormous amounts of food and pressuring Penelope.

4. Why does Penelope have suitors?

The suitors insist Odysseus must be dead and Penelope should marry one of them.

5. What advice does Athena give to Telemachus?

Athena advises Telemachus to grow up and take charge, send the suitors home, and go on a search for news of his father.

Answer these questions as you read.

Book II
1. What trick does Penelope play on her suitors?

She tells them to wait until she has woven a shroud, but she weaves by day and unravels by night.

2. How does Athena help Telemachus?

She gives him wise advice, encourages him, goes with him, gives him a ship, a crew, and a good wind.

Book III
1. How does Nestor feel about Odysseus?

Nestor admires Odysseus.

2. How does Nestor react when he realizes Athena is Telemachus' companion?

He offers prayers and sacrifices for her favor.

Book IV

1. How do Helen and Menelaus realize Telemachus is Odysseus' son?

He sheds tears over Odysseus' and resembles him.

2. How does Menelaus feel about Odysseus?

He loves him, admires him, and feels indebted to him.

3. How does Antinous plan to destroy Telemachus?

He plans to ambush his ship and kill him.

Book V

1. Who does Zeus send to Calypso?

Hermes

2. What is Hermes sent to do?

He's sent to tell Calypso to let Odysseus go home.

3. What can Hermes do with his wand?

He can put people to sleep or awaken them.

4. How does Calypso feel about Hermes' message?

She doesn't want to let Odysseus go, but she obeys.

5. What happens when Odysseus leaves?

Poseidon sends a terrible storm and batters Odysseus' raft.

6. What happens at the end of this book?

Odysseus washes ashore and falls asleep under the protection of some olive shoots.

Book VI

1. What does Athena influence Nausicaa to do while she sleeps?

She tells Nausicaa to wash her clothes and travel to the water by cart.

2. What wakes Odysseus?

The girls are playing ball and the ball goes into deep water, causing them all to shout. Their noise wakes Odysseus.

3. Why doesn't Nausicaa run away from Odysseus like the other girls?

Athena put courage in her heart.

4. What does Athena do for Odysseus after he bathes?

She makes him look taller and stronger and makes the hair on his head grow thick and long.

5. Why does Nausicaa make Odysseus follow behind the wagon?

She's afraid people will gossip and think poorly of her if they see Odysseus riding with her in the cart.

6. What does Nausicaa tell Odysseus to do if he wants her father's help?

She tells him to hide in her father's garden, then later go into town, ask for her father's house, and entreat her mother's favor.

Book VII

1. What are the Phaeacians best known for?

They are best known for shipping, and the women for weaving.

2. How do they treat Odysseus?

They treat him royally.

Lesson 46: The Odyssey Study Guide

Book VIII

1. What activities does King Alcinous use to entertain Odysseus?

He uses food, drink, song, games of sport, and dancing.

2. Who is Demodocus?

He's a blind bard who sings and plays the lute.

3. How does King Alcinous help Odysseus?

He gives him a ship and excellent sailors to take him home safely.

4. How does Odysseus react when Demodocus sings about the Trojan War?

He weeps.

Lesson 46: Verb Tense Agreement

If the tense in the underlined verbs matches, place a check mark in the blank. If the tense needs to be corrected, put an X in the blank and fix the problem.

X   If the game <u>starts</u> on time, it **will finish** before my meeting.

✓   I <u>am</u> bummed it's raining today because I <u>had planned</u> to play outside.

✓   Everyone <u>thought</u> the flower <u>would live</u> longer.

X   While we <u>visited</u> the zoo the giraffes **were eating**.

✓   Chase <u>wants</u> to show us the play he <u>wrote</u>.

Fill in the blanks with a verb that fits the tense. **(Answers will vary.)**

If the weather is warm enough, I want _____.

By the time my birthday rolls around, _____.

We left for the tournament as soon as _____.

When the final exams are graded, _____.

We gather together, wanting to _____.

Lesson 46: Verb/Subject Agreement Quiz

Choose the correct present tense verb for each sentence. When you're finished, check your answers and record your score out of 25.

1. Neither of those books _____ interesting to me.
   (a.) looks   b. look   c. looked   d. had looked

2. Cats and dogs chasing after him _____ William, but horses don't bother him.
   a. scares   **(b.) scare**   c. scared   d. had scared

3. Someone, maybe Holly or Liz, _____ the steps to solve the geometry problem.
   a. knew   **(b.) knows**   c. will know   d. know

4. The barking dogs and roaring train, coupled with the wind chimes playing in the wind each time it blows, _____ a noisy backdrop for the toddler's nap.
   a. made   b. has made   c. makes   **(d.) make**

5. The off brand soda _____ more than the on-sale name brand.
   (a.) costs   b. cost   c. will cost   d. had cost

6. Every pen and marker _____ run out of ink.
   a. will have   **(b.) has**   c. have   d. had

7. Not only my brother but also my friend's sisters _____ learned the song.
   a. will have   b. has   **(c.) have**   d. had

8. Either *Alias* or *Friends* _____ Jack's favorite TV show.
   a. was   b. were   c. are   **(d.) is**

(continued on next page)

Lesson 46: Verb/Subject Agreement Quiz (cont.)

9. Economics _____ become my favorite subject because it's easy for me.
   a. will have   **(b.) has**   c. have   d. had

10. There _____ the stack of papers I need you to file.
    (a.) is   b. are   c. was   d. were

11. Three cups of chopped cucumbers _____ like too much to me.
    a. seemed   b. had seemed   **(c.) seems**   d. seem

12. Where _____ the papers I left on the table?
    a. was   b. were   c. is   **(d.) are**

13. World Civilizations _____ been my hardest course this year.
    a. will have   **(b.) has**   c. have   d. had

14. The seven seats in our van _____ transportation for our eight-person family.
    a. complicated   b. will complicate   **(c.) complicate**   d. complicates

15. Everyone in the group, even Natalie and Caleb, _____ to go home early.
    a. wanted   b. have wanted   c. want   **(d.) wants**

16. At the local day care, all of the toddlers _____ right after lunch.
    a. napped   b. will nap   **(c.) nap**   d. naps

17. Two hundred and thirty dollars _____ too much to pay for the course.
    (a.) is   b. are   c. was   d. were

(continued on next page)

18. Mr. Ahlemeyer is one of those piano teachers who _____ on daily practice.

    a. insists   **(b.) insist**   c. insisted   d. has insisted

19. Where _____ the apples you wanted me to share?

    a. is   b. were   **(c.) are**   d. was

20. My mom and my dad _____ singing.

    a. enjoys   **(b.) enjoy**   c. enjoyed   d. will enjoy

21. Jessica's new pair of shoes _____ rubbed a blister on her feet.

    a. have   b. had   c. will have   **(d.) has**

22. The heavy traffic _____ maddening because I'm in a hurry.

    (a.) is   b. are   c. was   d. were

23. Each of the soccer players _____ the ball before lining up to start the game.

    (a.) touches   b. touch   c. touched   d. will touch

24. These pants _____ so wet that they won't have time to dry before we leave.

    a. is   **(b.) are**   c. has been   d. had been

25. Each first, second, third, and fourth grader _____ a part in the play.

    a. will have   b. had   c. have   **(d.) has**

Answer these questions as you read.

Book IX

1. What happened to someone who ate of the lotus?

They experienced forgetfulness of home and a desire to stay.

2. How heavy was the door of the Cyclops' cave?

The door was so heavy that 22 carts could not move it.

3. What does the Cyclops do instead of answering Odysseus?

He kills and eats two crew members.

4. Why doesn't Odysseus kill the Cyclops?

He realizes they can't move the rock away from the cave opening.

5. What gift does Odysseus give the Cyclops?

He gives him a gift of wine.

6. What "present" does the Cyclops offer in return?

He says he will eat Odysseus last.

7. How do the men sneak out of the cave?

They hide under the bellies of sheep.

(continued on next page)

---

8. What does Odysseus do after he escapes and returns to his ship?

He begins to taunt the Cyclops.

9. How does the Cyclops respond?

He tears the top off a high mountain and throws it at Odysseus's ship.

10. What did a prophet once prophesy about the Cyclops?

A prophet prophesied that the Cyclops would lose his sight by the hand of Odysseus.

11. What does the Cyclops ask of his father Poseidon?

He asks Poseidon to heal him and to give Odysseus much trouble on the way home and when he gets home.

Book X

1. Who is the god of wind?

Aeolus son of Hippotas.

2. What favor does he do for Odysseus?

He binds up the stormy winds in a sack.

3. What do some of the men do that undoes what Aeolus had done for them?

They open the sack thinking there's gold inside and they release the storms.

4. What did the Laestrygonians do?

They threw rocks at Odysseus and his men and speared them like fishes and took them home to eat them.

5. What did Circe do to some of the men?

She drugged them and turned them into pigs.

6. Where does Circe send Odysseus?

She sends him to Hades to perform certain rituals.

Lesson 49: The Odyssey Study Guide

Book XI

1. How does Odysseus call the souls of the dead to himself?

He offers sacrifices.

2. Who is Teiresias?

He is a seer.

3. What does Odysseus want from Teiresias?

He wants to know his fate.

4. What does Teiresias tell Odysseus about his fate?

He says it will be a hard trip home, but it will be possible for him to make it.

5. What should Odysseus do to the suitors?

He should take revenge and kill them.

6. With whom does Teiresias say Odysseus should make peace?

He should make peace with Poseidon.

7. How did Odysseus's mother die?

She died of longing for Odysseus.

Lesson 50: The Odyssey Study Guide

Book XII

1. What happens to those who hear the song of the Sirens?

They lose all desire for home and they just die listening to the song.

2. What does Circe instruct Odysseus to do to avoid hearing the Sirens?

She says his men should stuff their ears with wax and he should be tied to the mast.

3. How does Circe describe Scylla?

She describes her as a monster with 12 misshapen feet, six necks and heads, and three rows of teeth in each head.

4. Why does Odysseus need to avoid Charybdis?

She is a whirlpool that will devour Odysseus's ship if he gets too close.

5. What did Odysseus not tell his men, for fear they would quit rowing?

He did not tell them about Scylla.

6. What happened to Odysseus's men at the end of Book XII?

Odysseus told them repeatedly not to kill the cattle of the sun but they did it anyway while he was sleeping and they were killed for it.

Lesson 51: The Odyssey Study Guide

Book XIII

1. How was Odysseus's journey home from Scheria?

He slept soundly the entire way, even after they arrived and they lifted him out of the ship.

2. What does Poseidon want to do to the Phaeacian ship?

He wants to kill all the men in the ship and erect a mound around the city.

3. What does Alcinous decide because of Poseidon's wrath?

He decides not to take anybody else home and to offer sacrifices to Poseidon.

4. Why does Athena want to disguise Odysseus?

She wants to disguise him for his protection so he can best the suitors.

5. What does Athena tell Odysseus to do now that he has returned to Ithaca?

She tells him to wait at the swineherd's until she brings Telemachus.

Lesson 52: The Odyssey Study Guide

Book XIV

1. What is the swineherd's name?

Eumaeus

2. What does the disguised Odysseus tell the swineherd about himself?

He says Odysseus (himself) will return this very year and do vengeance on all those who are ill-treating his wife and son.

3. How is Odysseus disguised?

He is a beggar, an old man, with holey clothes and gray hair.

Book XV

1. How has Eumaeus proven his faithfulness in this and previous books?

He's taken care of his flocks and honored Odysseus's parents.

2. Who do you think will be the first person to know Odysseus for whom he really is?

(Answers will vary)

Book XVI

1. What does Telemachus call Eumaeus?

He calls him old friend.

2. What does Athena do for Odysseus's appearance?

She gives him nice clothes, a strong body, and a beautiful face and skin.

3. What does Telemachus think when Odysseus comes back in and his disguise is removed?

Telemachus thinks Odysseus is a god.

4. What do Odysseus and Telemachus plan to do?

They plan to take away the suitors' weapons and armor and hide them away, keeping two of them for themselves.

Book XVII

1. What does Telemachus tell Penelope to do when she sees that he has returned?

He tells her to wash her face, change her dress, go upstairs with her maids, and promise sacrifices to the gods if they'll grant revenge upon the suitors.

2. What does Theoclymenus prophesy to Penelope?

He says that Odysseus is already in Ithaca and will have revenge.

3. Who recognizes Odysseus immediately?

His dog, Argos, recognizes him immediately.

4. Who angers Odysseus?

Antinous

5. Why doesn't Odysseus tell his servants and wife who he is right away?

He wants to test their loyalty.

Book XVIII

1. Why does Odysseus fight Irus?

Irus is a beggar who wants to beg at Odysseus's house and doesn't want the "competition" of Odysseus begging there as well.

2. What does Penelope trick the suitors into giving her?

She tricks the suitors into giving her presents.

3. Other than Irus at the beginning, what other two characters anger Odysseus in this book?

Melantho and Eurymachus anger Odysseus.

Lesson 57: The Odyssey Study Guide

Answer these questions as you read.

Book XIX

1. Disguised as the beggar, what does Odysseus tell Penelope about her husband?

He tells her that he met Odysseus a long time ago and that he will be coming soon.

2. How does Euryclea recognize Odysseus?

She recognizes a scar on his leg.

3. What happened to Odysseus that left him with a scar on his leg?

A wild boar attacked him while he was hunting with his grandfather.

4. What is the tournament of axes?

Penelope is challenging the suitors to string Odysseus's bow and shoot an arrow through twelve axes like Odysseus used to do. That will be the suitor she chooses.

Lesson 58: The Odyssey Study Guide

Answer these questions as you read.

Book XX

1. Which two characters in this book treat Odysseus poorly because he is a beggar?

Melanthius the goatherd and Ctesippus treat Odysseus poorly.

2. Who, in contrast, is kind to Odysseus the beggar?

Philoetius is kind to Odysseus.

3. What do you think Odysseus is going to do to the suitors?

(Answers will vary)

Lesson 59: The Odyssey Study Guide

Answer these questions as you read.

Book XXI

1. To whom does Odysseus reveal himself to get help in defeating the suitors?

He reveals himself to Eumaeus and Philoetius.

2. Why do the suitors become very angry when Odysseus asks for a turn to try to string the bow?

They fear he will succeed and shame them.

3. How is the beggar finally revealed to be Odysseus?

He successfully strings the bow and shoots the targets.

Lesson 60: The Odyssey Study Guide

Book XXII

1. Whom does Odysseus kill first? Why do you think he chose him?

He kills Antinous. He seemed to be the leader and had mocked Odysseus the beggar relentlessly.

2. What does Eurymachus claim once he realizes who Odysseus really is?

He claims that everything was Antinous's fault.

3. Who is caught taking weapons from the storeroom? What happens to him?

Melanthius is caught taking weapons. They bind him and hang him from the rafters.

4. Which servant begs to be spared? What second servant does Telemachus say should also be spared?

Phemius the minstrel begs to be spared. Telemachus says he is guiltless, as well as Medon who was good to him when he was a boy.

5. How does Odysseus figure out which of the maids have misconducted themselves?

Odysseus asks Euryclea to send them to him.

6. What does Odysseus do to the unfaithful maids?

He has them help clean up the mess the battle has created, and then he has them hanged.

7. What happens to Melanthius?

He is violently killed.

Book XXIII
1. How does Penelope test Odysseus to make sure it's him?
She tells Euryclea to move his bed. He built it in a way that it can't be moved.

2. Why does Penelope test Odysseus?
She is so overcome with shock, she can't believe it's really him.

3. What is the last task that Teiresias told Odysseus to complete? What will be his reward?
He has to travel a long distance and make a sacrifice to Poseidon. His reward will be a long, happy life.

4. What does Odysseus leave to do? What does he tell Penelope to do?
He leaves to go see his father. He tells Penelope to stay upstairs with the women, to see nobody, and to ask no questions.

Book XXIV
1. How does Odysseus prove his identity to Laertes?
He shows him his scar and tells how he got it before sharing other memories.

2. What is Laertes afraid will happen?
He's afraid the townspeople will seek revenge for the death of the suitors.

3. Who comes to get revenge on Odysseus?
The families of the slain suitors.

4. Whom does Laertes kill?
He kills Eupiethes, the father of Antinous.

5. Who stops the battle?
Athena stops the battle.

| Laestrygonians   Circe   Pig   Aeolus   Cyclops   Lotus-Eaters |

1. Gives Odysseus a bag containing all the winds.   **Aeolus**

2. Witch-goddess who lives in Aeaea.   **Circe**

3. The one-eyed monster through whose land they sail.   **Cyclops**

4. A group of giants.   **Laestrygonians**

5. In their land, some of Odysseus's men ate the plants and forgot about going home.   **Lotus-Eaters**

6. Circe turns Odysseus's men into these.   **Pigs**

| beeswax   Calypso   Charybdis   Hermes   Scylla   Sirens |

1. Tells Odysseus to resist Circe by eating herb candy.   **Hermes**

2. Six-headed monster who swallows sailors.   **Scylla**

3. Odysseus returns to Circe, buries his man, then sails past these.   **Sirens**

4. Odysseus uses this to plug ears against the Sirens.   **beeswax**

5. Zeus punishes Odysseus and he ends up with no crew on her island.   **Calypso**

6. A giant whirlpool that the ship encounters.   **Charybdis**

| old beggar   Tiresias   home   Penelope   bed   Telemachus |

1. Penelope finally believes Odysseus is her husband when he describes their _____.   **bed**

2. As we leave the Odyssey, Penelope remains here while Odysseus leaves to make his final journey.   **home**

3. When Odysseus returns to Ithaca, he is disguised as this.   **old beggar**

4. When he returns, _____ is fighting off suitors that have come to take control of his kingdom.   **Penelope**

5. Eumaeus and this person are the only two who know that the beggar is Odysseus.   **Telemachus**

6. Odysseus must leave to make one final journey to fulfill what the prophet _____ told him to do.   **Tiresias**

Take this test on *The Odyssey*. There are 33 multiple choice questions worth 1 point each and 3 essay questions worth 4 points each. Give yourself 5 points if you read the WHOLE thing and didn't skip any "books." This will give you a total of 50 possible points.

1. The *main* story of the Odyssey is

   a. Odysseus's influence with the gods   **c. Odysseus's heroic deeds**
   b. Odysseus's love of travel   d. Odysseus's loyalty

2. Which of these moments best demonstrates Odysseus's real, human side?

   a. He resists Circe's temptations   c. He refuses to taste the Lotus plant
   b. He weeps over his mother's ghost   d. He plugs his men's ears with beeswax

3. Which of these is an example of *simile*?

   a. Odysseus strung the bow in one motion.
   b. Odysseus watched the suitors like a captain surveying the angry sea.
   c. The suitors failed to string the bow.
   d. The Greek isles littering the ocean set the stage for the epic tale.

4. How do the Phaeacians help Odysseus?

   a. They give him a bag of winds.   c. They prophesy about his trip home.
   b. They provide him with food.   **d. They give him a ship and treasures.**

5. Through how many axes must the suitors shoot an arrow in Penelope's contest?

   a. thirty   .   c. eight
   b. twelve   d. seventeen

(continued on next page)

6. Which plant makes the sailors forget about wanting to return home?

   a. Lotus   c. Lily
   b. Hemlock   d. Poppy

7. Who or what is Argus?

   a. The leader of the suitors   c. The Cyclops
   b. Odysseus's old dog   d. A whirlpool

8. How does Euryclea recognize Odysseus?

   a. His voice   c. His eyes
   b. His craftiness   **d. His scar**

9. How does Odysseus safely listen to the Sirens' song?

   a. His men bind him to the ship's mast   c. He is protected by Athena
   b. He plugs his ears with beeswax   d. He eats a Lotus plant

10. How does Odysseus's mother die?

   a. old age   **c. grief**
   b. drowning   d. she's murdered

11. What does Tiresias warn Odysseus not to harm?

   a. the cattle of the Sun   c. the whirlpool
   b. the serpent   d. the Lotus plant

12. Who turns the sailors into pigs?

   a. Calypso   c. Scylla
   b. Poseidon   **d. Circe**

(continued on next page)

13. What does Odysseus do that angers Poseidon?

   a. disrespects the sea   c. attacks him
   b. blinds his son   d. tricks him with a disguise

14. Who rescues Odysseus from Calypso?

   a. Athena   c. Circe
   b. Nausicaa   **d. Hermes**

15. What does the death of Odysseus's dog emphasize?

   a. how long Odysseus has been gone   c. how loyal the dog is
   b. the dog doesn't love Odysseus   d. the dog is old

16. Where does Odysseus's journey take him (beginning and ending)?

   a. Sparta to Ithaca   **c. Troy to Ithaca**
   b. Sparta to Troy   d. Ithaca to Sparta

17. Which encounter does not result in the death of any of Odysseus's men?

   a. Laestrygonians   c. Scylla
   b. Lotus Eaters   d. Cyclops

18. Which of these places does Odysseus not visit?

   a. the realm of the gods   c. the island of cannibals
   b. the land of the dead   d. the cave of the Cyclops

19. Who was the last to find out that Odysseus was home?

   a. Penelope   c. Telemachus
   b. Laertes   d. Eumaeus

(continued on next page)

20. What is the name of the seer who returns to Ithaca with Telemachus?

   a. Theoclymenus   c. Eumaeus
   b. Tiresias   d. Laertes

21. Who offers Odysseus immortality?

   a. Athena   c. Circe
   b. Nausicaa   **d. Calypso**

22. Which god gave Odysseus a bag of winds?

   a. Poseidon   **c. Aeolus**
   b. Zeus   d. Hades

23. How many of Odysseus's men return to Ithaca with him?

   a. 0   c. 17
   b. 6   d. 10

24. Who awakens Odysseus while playing a game of ball?

   a. Arete   c. Euryclea
   b. Nausicaa   d. Athena

25. Who is the loyal swineherd?

   a. Melanthius   c. Eurystheus
   b. Demodocus   **d. Eumaeus**

26. Which of these best describes Penelope?

   a. stubborn   c. weak
   b. loyal   d. indecisive

(continued on next page)

27. Who prophesies a final task Odysseus must undertake?

   a. Theoclymenus   c. Eumaeus
   (b.) Tiresias   d. Laertes

28. From what war is Odysseus returning?

   a. Peloponnesian War   c. War with Sparta
   b. War on Mt. Olympia   (d.) Trojan War

29. For how many years is Odysseus held captive by Calypso?

   a. 20   c. 10
   (b.) 7   d. 1

30. How does Athena disguise Odysseus when he returns to Ithaca?

   (a.) a beggar   c. a child
   b. a suitor   d. a woman

31. For whom is Penelope weaving a shroud?

   (a.) Laertes   c. Odysseus
   b. Telemachus   d. Eumaeus

32. Who is Polyphemus?

   a. a Phaecean   c. a Lotus Eater
   b. Circe's servant   (d.) the Cyclops

33. What name does Odysseus give when he introduces himself to the Cyclops?

   a. Odysseus   (c.) Noman
   b. Zeus   d. Poseidon

(continued on next page)

Choose 3 questions to answer in a brief essay (paragraph). Support your answers with evidence from the story. Here's the rubric for these questions.

Answers will obviously vary. Here are some suggested guidelines.

1. Evidence they admire him: the situations in which he saves them from harm or death, the crew obeys his orders almost without exception; evidence they don't respect him: their acts in the land of the Cicones and the land of Helios.

2. Evidence he controls his own destiny: his heroic deeds, his ability to escape from life-threatening situations, he makes choices along the journey such as whether to stay with Calypso, whether to escape the Cyclops's cave or remain and face the challenge; evidence the gods control his fate: Zeus's control of the winds, Poseidon's grudge against him, Tiresias's predictions, Athena's hand in his successes.

3. Any number of options would be acceptable provided the student supported it with evidence.

4. Many options such as physical strength, mental quickness, bravery, leadership, perseverance, honesty, self-control, etc. All should be supported by examples from the story.

5. Again, any number of options would be acceptable provided the student supported it with evidence.

---

1. It's good that _____ can come with us.

   (a.) she   b. her   c. hers

2. You scratched _____ car.

   a. I   b. me   (c.) my

3. _____ scored more baskets than anyone else.

   (a.) He   b. Him   c. His

4. We should invite _____ to our game night.

   a. they   (b.) them   c. theirs

5. We decided that resting was in _____ best interest.

   a. we   b. us   (c.) our

6. Emily knew that it was up to _____ to get everyone to safety.

   a. she   (b.) her   c. hers

7. Would you like to come with _____ to the store?

   a. I   (b.) me   c. my

Choose the correct pronoun to fill in the blank. If you need help, try to determine if the needed pronoun should be a subject, object, or possessive pronoun.

It was _____ who folded all of that laundry.
   me   myself   (I)

My dad asked my brother and _____ to do our chores.
   (me)   myself   I

Meg and _____ spent the entire day playing cards.
   me   myself   (I)

My mom was not happy with _____ inviting several friends over without asking.
   me   myself   (my)

Between you and _____, that dinner could have been a lot better.
   (me)   myself   I

_____ spent all night on the phone together.
   (She and Melanie)   Melanie and her

_____ friendship is important to me.
   (Jennifer's and my)   Me and Jennifer's   Myself and Jennifer's

Are you upset with _____ choosing of the movie?
   me   myself   (my)

When it comes to haircuts, I like yours better than _____.
   (mine)   mines   mine's

Lesson 74: Pronouns

1. Either the teacher or your dad needs to give _____ permission.
   - (his)   their

2. With some effort, her stained shorts were restored to _____ clean condition.
   - its   (their)

3. Every one of the books was missing _____.
   - (its dust jacket)   their dust jackets

4. Both the book and the table got _____ cleaned after the spill.
   - its surface   (their surfaces)

5. Neither of my sisters put away _____ laundry today.
   - (her)   their

6. Each member of the men's group got to cast _____ vote.
   - (his)   their

7. Both the dog and the cat tried to assert _____ dominance.
   - its   (their)

8. The team of girls left _____ mark throughout the tournament.
   - (its)   their

Lesson 75: Pronouns

1. The family opted to cancel _____ family reunion when everyone got sick.
   - (its)   their

2. Either my sister or my aunts will offer _____ home for our meal.
   - her   (their)

3. Not only the mosquitoes but also that fly better not flap _____ wings in my ear anymore!
   - (its)   their

4. Each daughter, mother, and grandmother in attendance was recognized for _____ accomplishments.
   - (her)   their

5. That cat, as well as all of those dogs, better keep _____ paws off my lawn.
   - (its)   their

6. I need the scissors and I can't find _____.
   - it   (them)

7. Both Ethan and Caleb wanted _____ steak cooked medium well.
   - his   (their)

8. The committee decided to postpone _____ meeting.
   - (its)   their

Lesson 90: Character Matching

Do you know who these characters are? The list of possible answers is in the box. Use the internet to search if you don't know one.

Arthur	Guinevere	Merlin	Sir Gawain
Sir Kay	Sir Galahad	Sir Mordred	

Foster brother of King Arthur — **Sir Kay**

Illegitimate son of Arthur; traitor — **Sir Mordred**

Sat in the siege perilous; went on quest for Holy Grail — **Sir Galahad**

Knight of Arthur's court who was attractive and a ladies' man — **Sir Gawain**

Wife of King Arthur — **Guinevere**

Arthur's adviser and magician — **Merlin**

Great king of Britain — **Arthur**

Lesson 94: Parallel Form

Answer whether each sentence is parallel or not parallel. Record your score out of 9 (chance for an extra credit point).

1. He wanted to go to the post office and eating lunch.
   - parallel   (not parallel)

2. Ethan grabbed his keys, found his sunglasses, and left the house.
   - (parallel)   not parallel

3. Stuart was amazed at not only the sunset, but also the starry sky.
   - (parallel)   not parallel

4. Evelyn wants the chocolate chip cookie but also is wanting cake.
   - parallel   (not parallel)

5. The dog was furry, happy, and hyper.
   - (Parallel)   not parallel

6. She proposed that we go for a run and then we should stop for smoothies.
   - parallel   (not parallel)

7. When Amy gets home she likes either cooking dinner or to take a bath.
   - parallel   (not parallel)

8. My sister gave me not only a high five but also a hug when I fixed her lunch.
   - (Parallel)   not parallel

9. Some people say that being smart is the same thing as to get good grades.
   - parallel   (not parallel)

10. Did you choose to come in because it is raining or were you done playing?
    - parallel   (not parallel)

Lesson 96: Nonfiction • Biography

Match each example to the type of nonfiction it represents.

E 1. Article   A. Frederick Douglass wrote about his life

A 2. Autobiography   B. "Angela's Ashes" by Frank McCourt (recounts his Experiences during his impoverished childhood)

D 3. Biography   C. A principal addresses the student body of her school

F 4. Diary   D. A book about Edgar Allan Poe's life

B 5. Memoir   E. A New York Times Newspaper piece

C 6. Speech   F. Anne Frank's daily, chronological accounts of her experiences

Lesson 99: Parallelism

Choose whether each sentence is parallel or nonparallel.

1. Dustin ate broccoli, mashed potatoes, and skipped the turkey.

    parallel   **(not parallel)**

2. Elizabeth was making a grocery list, checked the fridge, and looked in the pantry before heading to the store.

    parallel   **(not parallel)**

3. Patricia types quickly, reads speedily, and forgets easily.

    (parallel)   not parallel

4. Bears that roar, growling leopards, and screeching eagles created a cacophony at the zoo.

    parallel   **(not parallel)**

5. Neither the pelting of the rain nor the blowing of the wind could keep Andrew from playing outside.

    (parallel)   not parallel

Choose the sentence from each group that is parallel.

6. ○ Janet is a mathematician but who works at the grocery store at night.
    ○ Stuart is loud, boisterous, and a hyper child.
    ● Stephanie not only walked the walk but also talked the talk.

7. ○ I always have read and will read nonfiction twice a month.
    ● Running, hiking, and skiing are Jenn's favorite outdoor activities.
    ○ Bird watching, relaxing, and a brisk walk are Holly's favorites.

8. ● I hope to visit either Rome or Paris.
    ○ By noon I want either to eat lunch or to be sleeping.
    ○ I desire either to run a marathon or swim a 100-meter freestyle race.

Lesson 102: Plagiarism Quiz

1. Plagiarism can be avoided by thoroughly citing sources.   **True**

2. Ideas cannot really be stolen.   **False**

3. You can use a "Works Cited" list for listing the sources you've used.   **True**

4. If you paraphrase or summarize a document, you don't have to cite the source.   **False**

5. Sometimes something popular, like playing covers of copyrighted songs, can still be considered plagiarism.   **True**

Lesson 102: Literary Terms Quiz

Take this quiz on literary terms. Record up to 10 points out of 5 (possible extra credit).

1. This refers to the struggle, usually between the protagonist and antagonist.
    a. setting   b. theme   **(c) conflict**

2. A character who tells a story is a _____.
    a. character   **(b) narrator**   c. antagonist

3. The protagonist is _____.
    (a) the main/central character, sometimes called the hero
    b. the character who opposes the main character, typically creating the conflict

4. A person or animal who takes part in the action of a literary work is a _____.
    (a) character   b. narrator   c. protagonist

5. The time and location in which the story takes place is the _____.
    a. point of view   **(b) setting**   c. theme

6. The antagonist is _____.
    a. the main/central character, sometimes called the hero
    (b) the character who opposes the main character, typically creating the conflict

7. The theme of a novel is _____.
    a. the struggle between characters   **(b) the main idea; point of the story**

8. The highest point of suspense or interest is the _____.
    a. rising action   b. resolution   **(c) climax**

9. A character who shows many different traits and faults is known as _____.
    a. simple   **(b) round**   c. dynamic

10. The end of the central conflict is the _____.
    (a) resolution   b. denouement   c. falling action

Write the correct forms of the possessive noun.

the one cats tail

__cat's__

the two birds wings

__birds'__

the mens room

__men's__

the many cars horns

__cars'__

the one trucks wheels

__truck's__

the five girls dresses

__girls'__

Read the following story. If the word preceding the blank is correctly written, put a check in the blank. If it's incorrect, put an x in the blank. Check your answers and record your score out of 25.

The Meier's __x__ are a family of four: Mom, Dad, and two girls. The Meiers' __✔__ favorite vacation spot is Disney World. Disneys' __x__ rooms hold up to four people so it work's __x__ out perfectly for the Meiers __✔__. They always drive down to Disney World. The tradition is to stop at McDonald's __✔__ for a hot breakfast in the early morning hour's __x__. Then they drive as far as they can before stopping again. The girls' __✔__ favorite thing to do on the road is to pop a Disney DVD into their vans' __x__ DVD player and plan out what rides they'll visit first. The family's __✔__ coin stash is always used up by the Florida toll's __x__, but it's a small price to pay for family fun. (One time, Mr. Meier forgot to roll down the driver's __✔__ window and tossed the quarters __✔__ straight into the glass. His two daughter's __x__ laughs lasted for several minutes after that.)

Once the familys' __x__ journey to Disney is complete, next comes the trek to the parks __✔__. They always start at the Magic Kingdom. As funny as it sounds, the trip on the buses __✔__ from the hotel is always an exciting part of the vacation for the Meier girls. The smell of the diesel fuel and the hissing of the brake's __x__ are quintessential Disney sights and smells for them. Upon arrival at the Magic Kingdom, the family heads straight for Main Streets' __x__ Confectionery for some sweet treats. The girls usually order childrens' __x__ sizes because they're still such large servings. Besides __✔__, they don't want to be too full when they finally get to ride the roller coaster's __x__.

After a long day in the Magic Kingdom of riding rides and indulging in theme park treats, the family likes to watch the fireworks __✔__ show. Set to various clips of Disney music, the booming explosions light up the night sky while lightly illuminating each of the Meiers' __✔__ happy faces. With happy hearts and exhausted feet __✔__, the family returns to wait for the bus to take them back to their hotel, eager for a night of restful sleep before they start it all over again in the morning.

Solve the crossword puzzle. There are no spaces between words.

Across:
2. the structure used to break down and display story elements
3. this introduces the characters and the conflicts in the story
7. the feeling conveyed to readers by events, characters, setting, etc. in a story
8. events that unfold after the exposition; conflicts progress leading up to the climax

Down:
1. action begins to wrap up; concluding events
4. the ending of the story; loose ends are tied up here
5. another name for resolution
6. the turning point; point of maximum interest or highest tension of the story

Take the quiz and record your score on your grade sheet.

1. In "A Hunger Artist," the _____ in this story symbolizes the hunger artist's separation from society.
   a. paintbrush
   (b.) cage
   c. artist

2. What is the maximum fasting limit the impresario will allow for the hunger artist?
   (a.) 40 days
   b. 10 days
   c. 30 days

3. How does the hunger artist die?
   a. He dies from loneliness.
   (b.) He dies from starvation in a cage with little notice.
   c. He dies at the hands of another artist.

4. What takes the place of the hunger artist in the cage?
   a. lion
   b. tiger
   (c.) panther

Lesson 115: Short Story Terms Quiz

Take this short story terms quiz. Record your score out of 6 (potential for extra credit).

character	characterization	direct characterization
dynamic character	flat character	indirect characterization
narrative	round character	short story	static character

A fully-developed character about whom the reader knows much — **round character**

when a character's personality is revealed through actions or hints — **indirect characterization**

a character the reader doesn't know very well/isn't very developed — **flat character**

the process of revealing a character's personality — **characterization**

a narrative that's typically ten to twenty pages — **short story**

a changing character – one who grows and learns as the story goes on — **dynamic character**

a literary work that tells a story — **narrative**

a person or animal in a literary work — **character**

a character that remains steady and does not change throughout the story — **static character**

when the reader knows what a character's personality is like — **direct characterization**

Lesson 122: Sentence Structures

Choose whether each sentence below is simple, compound, or complex. Check your answers and record your score.

1. My brother likes grape jelly, and my sister likes strawberry jelly.
   a. simple sentence **(b.) compound sentence** c. complex sentence

2. An independent clause connected to a dependent clause makes a ____.
   a. simple sentence b. compound sentence **(c.) complex sentence**

3. The sky looks nasty, so I'd better grab my raincoat.
   a. simple sentence **(b.) compound sentence** c. complex sentence

4. While his mom napped, Justin cleaned the kitchen.
   a. simple sentence b. compound sentence **(c.) complex sentence**

5. Bryce and Bristol read a book together all afternoon.
   (a.) simple sentence b. compound sentence c. complex sentence

6. Mom could not find the car keys although she searched the whole house.
   a. simple sentence b. compound sentence **(c.) complex sentence**

7. An independent clause that stands alone is a _____.
   (a.) simple sentence b. compound sentence c. complex sentence

8. Two independent clauses connected to each other with a conjunction.
   a. simple sentence **(b.) compound sentence** c. complex sentence

9. The sponsor of the sporting event plastered their logo on every surface.
   (a.) simple sentence b. compound sentence c. complex sentence

10. The song played on the radio before we arrived at the concert.
    a. simple sentence b. compound sentence **(c.) complex sentence**

Lesson 123: Poetic Devices

Identify which poetic device is being used in each example. Your choices are in the word box (some words are used more than once).

alliteration	hyperbole	idiom	metaphor
onomatopoeia	personification	rhyme	simile

The wind bit my nose as it roared. — **personification**

The sweet, silly sisters scaled the stairs. — **alliteration**

Your room is a pigsty! — **metaphor**

Tick tock goes the clock. — **onomatopoeia**

A fat cat sat on my hat. — **rhyme**

It's raining cats and dogs today. — **idiom**

Her skin was like silky milk chocolate. — **simile**

That was the easiest question in the world. — **hyperbole**

Time marches on, despite our objections. — **personification**

I'm so hungry I could eat a horse! — **hyperbole**

The snow was a blanket covering the ground. — **metaphor**

I think I bit off more than I can chew. — **idiom**

Her hands were as cold as ice. — **simile**

Lesson 128: Poetic Devices Crossword

Complete the crossword puzzle.

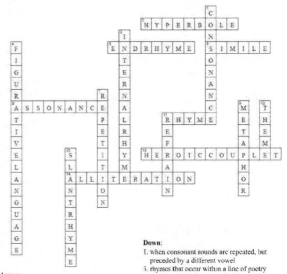

Across:
2. an extreme exaggeration to make a point
5. rhymes that have the same ending sounds (ex. stay and way)
6. a comparison between two things using "like" or "as"
8. repetition of vowel sounds
11. repetition of the end sounds of words
13. two rhymed lines in iambic pentameter
14. repetition of beginning consonant sounds

Down:
1. when consonant sounds are repeated, but preceded by a different vowel
3. rhymes that occur within a line of poetry
4. any type of writing that takes the words beyond their literal meaning
7. when a word, phrase, line, or stanza is repeated in a poem
9. a comparison between two unlike things, saying one thing IS another
10. the main idea in a work of literature
11. a repeated part of a poem, particularly at the end of a stanza, or between stanzas
12. rhyme that are close, but not exact

Lesson 128: Sentence Types Quiz

Choose whether each sentence below is simple, compound, or complex.

1. Rebecca stayed in bed because she was sick.
   a. simple sentence   b. compound sentence   **c. complex sentence**

2. Please hand me the remote.
   a. simple sentence   b. compound sentence   c. complex sentence

3. Kaitlyn wants to play a game, so I'm going to play one with her.
   a. simple sentence   **b. compound sentence**   c. complex sentence

4. If you want to have dessert, you'll have to finish your dinner.
   a. simple sentence   b. compound sentence   **c. complex sentence**

5. Look out!
   a. simple sentence   b. compound sentence   c. complex sentence

6. Although we tried our best, we didn't win the three-legged race.
   a. simple sentence   b. compound sentence   **c. complex sentence**

7. Traci wants to come over, but she hasn't finished her homework.
   a. simple sentence   **b. compound sentence**   c. complex sentence

8. When Chase grows up, he wants to be an engineer.
   a. simple sentence   b. compound sentence   **c. complex sentence**

9. The light turned red before we got through the intersection.
   a. simple sentence   b. compound sentence   **c. complex sentence**

10. Natalie wants a pet bunny, but she doesn't know how to care for it.
    a. simple sentence   **b. compound sentence**   c. complex sentence

Lesson 142: Subject/Verb Agreement Quiz

Choose the correct present tense verb for each sentence. When you're finished, check your answers and record your score out of 25.

1. Each man, woman, and child _____ food and shelter.
   a. will need   b. need   **c. needs**   d. needed

2. Politics _____ made friends into enemies.
   a. has   b. have   c. will have   d. had

3. Alice's, famous for delicious club sandwiches, _____ developed a new sandwich.
   a. is   b. had   c. have   **d. has**

4. Every cucumber, zucchini, and pepper from the garden _____ amazing.
   a. tasted   b. has tasted   **c. tastes**   d. taste

5. All of my favorite foods _____ on sale this week.
   a. is   **b. are**   c. was   d. were

6. There _____ Stephanie and Ben on their bikes.
   a. went   b. has gone   c. goes   **d. go**

7. Not only the Andersons but also Lindsay _____ tried the new deli.
   a. will have   **b. has**   c. have   d. had

8. There _____ more papers to be filed than you think.
   a. was   b. were   **c. are**   d. is

(continued on next page)

Lesson 142: Subject/Verb Agreement Quiz (cont.)

9. Raking leaves into piles taller than me _____ Kim, my hardworking daughter.
   a. is   b. are   c. was   d. were

10. Johnson and Johnson _____ a baby shampoo with a nostalgic smell.
    a. makes   b. make   c. made   d. have made

11. Neither the encyclopedias nor the dictionary _____ the word I'm looking for.
    a. had   b. will have   c. have   **d. has**

12. Not only the clouds but also the shade _____ it feel colder under the tree.
    a. made   b. make   **c. makes**   d. will make

13. The jury _____ to adjourn for the day.
    a. are wanting   **b. wants**   c. wanted   d. want

14. _____ no one except Andy and Bev remember the answer to the riddle?
    a. Has   b. Did   **c. Does**   d. Do

15. Ten dollars _____ a lot of money to spend on a single lunch.
    a. is   b. are   c. was   d. were

16. The sisters, along with Bradley, _____ to avoid the traffic by leaving early.
    a. hoped   b. will hope   **c. hope**   d. hopes

17. Neither of my parents _____ attending the meeting.
    a. is   b. are   c. was   d. were

(continued on next page)

Lesson 142: Subject/Verb Agreement Quiz (cont.)

18. Here _____ the sandwich and chips you ordered.
    a. is   **b. are**   c. was   d. were

19. My dog, together with my cat, _____ to lay on the heater vents in the winter.
    a. likes   b. like   c. liked   d. had liked.

20. Each of my brothers _____ a different sport.
    a. enjoys   b. enjoy   c. enjoyed   d. will enjoy

21. On the hill _____ many rocks that slow our biking progress.
    a. is   **b. are**   c. was   d. were

22. Jessica is one of those girls who _____ long hair.
    a. liked   b. likes   **c. like**   d. has liked

23. A donut with sprinkles _____ more fun than one without sprinkles.
    a. were   b. was   c. are   **d. is**

24. There already _____ skaters at the rink.
    a. is   **b. are**   c. has been   d. had been

25. Measles _____ about two weeks.
    a. will last   b. lasted   c. last   **d. lasts**

Lesson 146: Prepositional Phrase Quiz

Underline the prepositional phrases in each sentence below. Some sentences have more than one prepositional phrase.

1. The neighbors <u>across the street</u> lost their tree <u>in a storm</u>.

2. <u>At the stroke</u> <u>of midnight</u>, I will be thirteen years old.

3. I've met three different Jennifers <u>since Tuesday</u>.

4. My meatball rolled <u>under the table</u>.

5. <u>Before your first day</u>, make sure you know the requirements <u>of the job</u>.

6. It was <u>beyond me</u> why anyone wanted to ride <u>on the spinning rides</u>.

7. We got lost <u>along the way</u>, but we finally found the route <u>to the house</u>.

8. He beat me <u>to the park</u> <u>by running</u> the whole way.

9. There was a massive wind storm <u>during the night</u>.

10. We took a touristy picture <u>outside Buckingham Palace</u>.

11. I was busy all day <u>between cooking and cleaning</u>.

12. When we lined up <u>against the wall</u>, I was <u>behind my brother</u>.

13. Let's not go <u>down that rabbit trail</u>.

14. Do you want to come <u>with me</u> <u>to the library</u>?

15. Did you check <u>beside the computer</u>?

Lesson 152: Emma Quiz

Take this quiz on Emma. Record your score out of 10 (potential for extra credit).

1. Emma lives in Hartfield with...
   - a. her father and sister
   - **(b.) her father**
   - c. her father, sister, and governess
   - d. her father and mother

2. What does Frank Churchill do for Harriet?
   - a. He defends her against Augusta's attacks.
   - b. He marries her and she doesn't have to become a governess.
   - **(c.) He saves her from gypsies.**
   - d. He gives her money for a debt.

3. As the novel begins, whom has Emma matched with her neighbor, Mr. Weston?
   - a. Isabella, her sister
   - b. Harriet, her friend
   - c. Augusta Hawkins, her acquaintance
   - **(d.) Miss Taylor, her governess**

4. Whom does Mr. Weston think that George Knightly is fond of?
   - **(a.) Jane Fairfax**
   - b. Harriet
   - c. Augusta Hawkins
   - d. Miss Bates

5. What incident causes George Knightly to think Frank Churchill is a "trifling, silly fellow"?
   - a. His excessive flirting with Augusta at the dance
   - b. His purchase of a pianoforte
   - **(c.) His travelling to London for a haircut**
   - d. His insistence at having a ball at the Crown Inn

6. When Harriet says she is interested in someone above her station, whom does Emma think she is referring to?
   - a. Mr. Knightly
   - b. Mr. Martin
   - **(c.) Mr. Churchill**
   - d. Mr. Weston

7. Who says this line: "Better to be without sense than to misapply it as you do"?
   - a. Emma
   - b. Harriet
   - c. Frank Churchill
   - **(d.) George Knightly**

(continued on next page)

Lesson 152: Emma Quiz (cont.)

8. Which of the following couples are NOT engaged by the end of the book?
   - **(a.) Miss Bates and Mr. Perry**
   - b. Emma and Mr. Knightly
   - c. Harriet and Mr. Martin

9. What does George Knightly do for Harriet?
   - a. He saves her from gypsies.
   - b. He gives her advice not to marry Robert Martin.
   - **(c.) He asks her to dance when Mr. Elton ignores her.**
   - d. He saves her from her water-surrounded carriage.

10. How does Emma's first match for Harriet end?
   - **(a.) Mr. Elton falls in love with Emma and then marries Augusta.**
   - b. Mr. Elton's family won't give consent.
   - c. Augusta shows up and claims she is betrothed to Mr. Elton
   - d. Harriet rejects Mr. Elton's pursuit of her.

11. Why is Emma upset when she finds out Harriet has feelings for Mr. Knightly?
   - a. Emma wanted Mr. Knightly to marry Jane Fairfax.
   - **(b.) Emma loves Mr. Knightly.**
   - c. Emma had promised Harriet to Mr. Churchill.
   - d. Emma doesn't think Mr. Knightly is respectable.

12. Why does Emma not think Robert Martin is a good match for Harriet?
   - a. He is not titled.
   - b. He lives with his family.
   - **(c.) He is not proper enough.**
   - d. Mr. Knightly doesn't trust him.

13. For what does George Knightly reprimand Emma?
   - a. Her love of dancing
   - b. The way she treats her father
   - c. Her disrespect of Mrs. Weston's position
   - **(d.) Her rudeness at a picnic to Miss Bates**

Lesson 163: Much Ado About Nothing Quiz

Take this quiz on Much Ado About Nothing. Record your score out of 10 (potential for extra credit).

1. Who wants to marry Hero at the start of the play?
   - a. Don John
   - **(b.) Claudio**
   - c. Benedick
   - d. Don Pedro

2. What happens to Hero when Don John sets her up?
   - a. She goes insane.
   - b. She marries Benedick.
   - c. She runs away.
   - **(d.) She dies.**

3. Which of these best describes Beatrice?
   - a. She's naïve.
   - **(b.) She speaks her mind without worrying about etiquette.**
   - c. She is the play's biggest flirt.

4. Which character is the biggest flirt?
   - a. Ursula
   - **(b.) Margaret**
   - c. Beatrice
   - d. Hero

5. Whom does Claudio agree to marry after splitting up with Hero?
   - a. Beatrice
   - b. Margaret
   - **(c.) Antonio's daughter**
   - d. Ursula

6. Whom does Antonio tell Leonato is in love with Hero?
   - a. Benedick
   - **(b.) Don Pedro**
   - c. Don John
   - d. Claudio

7. What is Leonato?
   - a. a war hero
   - b. a constable
   - **(c.) a governor**
   - d. a king

(continued on next page)

8. Who is the constable's constant companion?

   a. Verges   b. Balthasar   c. Conrade

9. How do Don John and Boracio decide to disrupt Hero and Claudio's marriage?

   a. By making Hero appear to be disrespectful of her family
   b. By making Claudio appear to be dead
   c. By making Hero appear to be cheating on Claudio

10. Who provides the most comic relief in the play?

   a. Conrade   b. Don John   **c. Dogberry**   d. Leonato

11. Who works to bring Benedick and Beatrice back together?

   a. Claudio   **b. Don Pedro**   c. Boracio   d. Conrade

12. Why is Beatrice so rude to Benedick?

   a. She doesn't trust men.   **c. He hurt her in the past.**
   b. She is a snob.   d. She doesn't want to marry.

13. Do Hero and Claudio eventually get married?

   a. yes   b. no

14. Who says, "A man loves the meat in his youth, that he cannot endure in his age"?

   a. Benedick   b. Don John   c. Don Pedro   d. Claudio

15. Why does Don John dislike his brother, Don Pedro?

   a. He lost to Don Pedro in battle   c. Don Pedro is the sole heir
   b. Don Pedro feels sorry for Don John   **d. all of these**

Take your final exam. It is worth 100 points: 50 vocabulary questions each worth 1 point, 25 multiple choice questions each worth 1 point, and 5 essay questions each worth 5 points. Record your score on your grade sheet.

Circle the letter that contains the word that best fits.

1. The _____ of animal noises gave me a headache.

   a. cacophony   b. longevity   c. demeanor   d. veracity

2. His _____ behavior earned him the respect of the squad.

   a. fraudulent   b. insidious   **c. exemplary**   d. sacrosanct

3. Sometimes quiet people become quite _____ when they're nervous.

   a. nautical   **b. loquacious**   c. abstract   d. translucent

4. A synonym for shy.

   a. docile   b. rebuke   **c. demure**   d. integrity

5. The _____ between a boy and his dog is unparalleled.

   a. congregation   b. fuse   c. orator   **d. camaraderie**

6. Our _____ lives have made us forget how to appreciate art.

   a. prosaic   b. recalcitrant   c. intransigent   d. lucrative

7. Don't _____ your sister, get along!

   a. anticipate   **b. antagonize**   c. depict   d. transmute

8. The clerk wouldn't cash the _____ check.

   a. impassive   b. pertinacious   c. recalcitrant   **d. fraudulent**

9. A synonym for annoy.

   a. transmute   **b. vex**   c. anticipate   d. oppose

10. An antonym of concrete.

   a. abstract   b. impassive   c. submissive   d. propitious

---

11. The _____ teenager gets into trouble often.

   a. lucrative   b. nautical   **c. recalcitrant**   d. impassive

12. The politician created an ad to _____ his opponent.

   a. generalize   **b. vilify**   c. expiate   d. adhere

13. The juror had the _____ to challenge the expert's opinion.

   a. effrontery   b. prosperity   c. constituent   d. connotation

14. You should not _____ your own worth.

   a. expiate   **b. deprecate**   c. generalize   d. expunge

15. The girl gave a _____ shrug.

   a. trilateral   b. sanctimonious   c. vicarious   **d. nonchalant**

16. The fur coat was a bit _____ for the funeral.

   a. intuitive   b. consecutive   **c. ostentatious**   d. trenchant

17. Will the Florida _____ be joining the assembly?

   a. grandeur   b. invective   **c. contingent**   d. surfeit

18. The _____ display got us all in the Christmas spirit.

   a. jubilant   b. clairvoyant   c. redundant   d. circuitous

19. The aspirin served to _____ his pain.

   a. impute   **b. palliate**   c. surfeit   d. reflect

20. The drama queen behaved in a _____ way toward even the smallest incident.

   a. prudent   b. incompatible   **c. maudlin**   d. inchoate

21. The newspaper's _____ of the rally infuriated its organizers.

   a. invective   b. contingent   c. grandiloquence   d. panacea

22. The scientist had a _____ approach to dealing with the water shortage.

   a. pragmatic   b. prurient   c. facetious   d. correlate

---

23. The _____ inquiry about my health was appreciated.

   a. unilateral   b. skeptical   **c. solicitous**   d. incongruous

24. The _____ of business owners sponsored a scholarship.

   a. differential   **b. coalition**   c. jurisdiction   d. sycophant

25. Playing in the basketball game left me _____.

   a. parched   b. precipitous   c. relevant   d. incongruous

26. The _____ mess of a room took hours to clean.

   a. pugnacious   b. incontrovertible   c. sustainable   **d. jumbled**

27. We were _____ to the trail of ants coming in overnight.

   a. uninspired   **b. oblivious**   c. haughty   d. obsequious

28. The _____ didn't gel as much as the chemist had anticipated.

   a. solution   b. compassion   c. criterion   d. pariah

29. Splitting all the candy was the most _____ thing I could think of.

   a. fastidious   b. fallacious   c. indefatigable   **d. equitable**

30. The toddler didn't want to _____ his sister's toy.

   a. preclude   b. collaborate   **c. relinquish**   d. justify

31. With _____ studying, he received a great score on the SAT.

   a. solipsistic   b. taciturn   **c. diligent**   d. uninspired

32. The desire to belong is a _____ one.

   a. qualitative   **b. primeval**   c. tedious   d. pretentious

33. The _____ box was hard to get through the door.

   a. tactile   b. latent   **c. cumbersome**   d. resilient

34. As _____ as it sounds, I prefer dining at country clubs.

   a. pretentious   b. obsolete   c. quanlitative   d. anachronistic